# THE
# SHADOW
# KING

*For dearest Bill
With my love!
Lidro*

## By Sidra Stone, Ph.D., and Hal Stone, Ph.D.

### BOOKS
Embracing Our Selves*
Embracing Each Other*
Embracing Your Inner Critic

### AUDIOCASSETTES
**Voice Dialogue: Relationships and the Psychology of Selves**
Making Relationships Work for You
Meeting Your Selves
The Dance of the Selves in Relationship
Understanding Your Relationships
The Child Within
The Voice of Responsibility
Meet the Pusher
Meet Your Inner Critic
Meet Your Inner Critic II
The Patriarch Within
Children & Marriage
Affairs & Attractions
Our Lost Instinctual Heritage
The Pleaser: Queen of the Primary Selves
The Rational Mind: King of the Primary Selves

**Voice Dialogue Training Tapes**
Introducing Voice Dialogue
Voice Dialogue Demonstrations

**The Dream Process**
Decoding Your Dreams
Exploring the Dark Side in Dreams

### VIDEOCASSETTES
The Inner Critic in Action
The Total Self
Ending the Tyranny of the Inner Patriarch

Items with asterisks (*) are available through Nataraj Publishing:
800-949-1091.

For all other items and workshop information, call Delos
(707) 937-2424, or fax (707) 937-4119.
E-mail: delos@mcn.org/                Website: http://delos-inc.com/

# THE
# SHADOW KING

The Invisible Force That Holds Women Back

Sidra Stone, Ph.D.

NATARAJ

Nataraj Publishing
Mill Valley, CA

Published in the United States by:
Nataraj Publishing
P.O. Box 2430
Mill Valley, CA 94942
(415) 388-7195

Designed by: Highpoint, Inc., Claremont, CA
Photo of Sidra Stone on back cover by: Antonia Lamb
Front cover artwork/design by: Judith Brown

Library of Congress Catalog Card number: 96-72596

ISBN 1-882591-31-3

00 99 98 97    4 3 2 1
First Printing, February 1997
Printed in the United States of America

This book is for every woman who has put aside
her own wisdom, deferred to others,
and waited for permission to speak.

It is also for her sister, the woman of power,
who has learned how to speak up,
but fears that in doing this she has sacrificed
some intangible but
precious aspect of her essential femininity.

To Hal

Whose wisdom, strength, and support
have contributed so much to women
and
whose love
gave me the courage and the safety
I needed
to meet the Shadow King

# CONTENTS

# ACKNOWLEDGMENTS

My heartfelt thanks to the many women and men who, over the years, have shared your Voice Dialogue sessions, dreams, insights, and ideas. You have provided the material from which this work with the Inner Patriarch has evolved. Although I cannot thank each of you personally, you have given us a priceless gift.

For my colleagues around the world who have brought this work into their own lives and teachings, I thank you for the exciting interchange of ideas and your support. It was wonderful to have you out there, exploring the Inner Patriarch in depth, teaching others about him, and sharing your observations with me.

I cannot mention everyone individually, but I would like to thank a number of people who have made specific contributions.

First of all, I would like to thank Marian van Riemsdijk, who was there in Holland at the very beginning and has gone on to develop her own powerful approach to this work.

Veeta Gensberger in Germany and Robin Gale and Di Scambler in Australia have supported me personally with their feedback and information and have had a real impact on the lives of women as they taught about the Inner Patriarch in their own parts of the world. Susan Schwartz in Norway has sent me her own keen observations over the years, which have enriched my perspective.

In the United States, Judith Tamar Stone in Los Angeles has emphasized the powerful role that the Inner Patriarch plays in relationships. Dassie Hoffman in New York has concentrated on the interactions of Inner Patriarch and Aphrodite. Miriam Dyak in Seattle has contributed general information, ideas, enthusiasm, and humor. Judith Hendin in Wilkes-Barre has explored, taught, written poetry, and given powerful dance performances using her own and others' Inner Patriarchs as inspiration. Among all these women, there is one man, John Cooper of Chicago, who over the years has continued to show a particular interest in this work and who suggested that I pay some well-deserved attention to the Inner Matriarch.

There is a group of dear friends and colleagues who have contributed much to the writing of this book. I would like to thank Shakti Gawain, Jim Burns, and Jane Hogan for their unflagging encouragement from the very beginning. Then, when the book was written, it was wonderful to have Carolyn Conger, Shakti Gawain, Hal Bennett, and Susan Swallow read the manuscript and give me their great ideas for enhancing it. I loved working with all of you. Thanks, too, to Lora O'Connor for her enthusiasm and hard work in shaping the book and getting it out into the world; Jill Kramer for overseeing the production; and Mary Lou Brewer for her work in creating a space for me to put it all together.

Last, but certainly not least, my thanks to Hal, my husband, my partner, and my best friend, without whom this book would never have been written!

I was winning the game of Anagrams and I loved it! I could feel my mind working like a powerful machine as I easily outdistanced the boy who faced me across the small table. I felt like Atalanta, a Greek heroine I admired at that time. She could run faster than anyone, man or woman, and I wanted to be just like her. But our mothers passed the room in which we were playing and, as they looked inside, they could see what was happening. My mother called me aside and whispered to me in a conspiratorial voice: "Let him win, dear, it will make him feel good. You know, boys don't like to lose to girls." So I went back to our game of Anagrams, and I dutifully lost it. My mother, in all good faith, was teaching me the subtle rules I would be expected to follow for the remainder of my life. She was helping to create my Inner Patriarch, who would rule over my behavior as a woman.

There have been many changes for women in the 50 years since this game of Anagrams was interrupted. Women are now allowed to win. We do not speak to our daughters the way my mother spoke to me. The rules have been changed. Thanks to the activities of the feminists, both men and women, the playing field is far more even than in the past. The patriarchal system that dominated our culture has been questioned and has undergone major alterations. There is still work to be done, but this book is not about changing the system.

This book is about changing ourselves. Although the outer system has been somewhat changed, many of our unconscious belief systems have not. Within each of us lives an Inner Patriarch that continues to carry the old patriarchal rules and values, many of which may have been taught us by our mothers. This Inner Patriarch controls us from the inside, not the outside. We do not necessarily know about him because he operates beyond the edges of our awareness. He rules from the shadows of our unconscious, which is why I sometimes call him the Shadow King. When we do not know about him, this Shadow King is our enemy.

*The enemy is no longer "out there" but lies deep within each of us.* This is actually very advantageous. Because we are dealing with our own beliefs rather than the beliefs of others, we, as individuals, have the power to make whatever changes we wish.

### About This Book

This book is primarily written for women, but it is valuable for men as well. Not only will men learn about their own Patriarchs, but they will certainly gain a greater understanding of the women in their lives.

This book provides the information and the tools you will need to discover your own Inner Patriarch and to change him. It shines a light into the unconscious where the Shadow King reigns so that you can discover your own beliefs and begin to evaluate them consciously. It then presents effective tools for making the changes that you want to make.

The first section of the book introduces you to the Shadow King. It gives a picture of his subtle influence upon us as women and upon values of the culture in which we live. I describe my initial meetings with this Shadow King, or Inner Patriarch, and give an overview of who he is and how he functions. The second section of the book is devoted to an in-depth study of the Inner Patriarch as I have come to know him. The third section shows how we women have dealt with him in the past. The remainder of the book is devoted to a new way of dealing with the Inner Patriarch. It includes both an appreciation of his gifts and a number of effective methods that will change him from an enemy into an ally. It ends with a new path to follow, one which will allow full and creative partnership between men and women.

## Background

I have spent many years studying this elusive ruler. I have had my own personal experiences with him, and I have spoken with thousands of women and men about their Inner Patriarchs. The material in this book is drawn from direct experience. (I have changed the names of the people involved to protect their privacy.)

As I came to know my own Inner Patriarch and those of other women, a clear pattern emerged. *I could see how our Patriarchs keep us in an inferior position—if not at our work, then in our relationships. They make us distrust ourselves. Even more important was the discovery that they make us distrust other women as well.* They trust and value men, and those traditionally male qualities, more than women and anything traditionally feminine.

I saw again and again how the Inner Patriarch devalued us and what we did just because we were women. Although we have the right to expect equal pay for equal work (even if this is not always forthcoming), we have not yet reached the point at which we can casually *give ourselves* equal recognition for equal work. Our Inner Patriarchs give men greater recognition for their accomplishments than they give us. *What we do is just not as important as what a man does; if a man had done the same piece of work, it would be considered more important. This is true both for our accomplishments and for those of other women.* There is nothing personal in this; the Inner Patriarchs feel the same about all women and about all things womanly.

In my early years, my greatest pride was that I was not like other women. I was better than other women because I was more like a man. I was a professional woman, a sensible, hardworking high achiever who would never let her feelings slow her down. Before I had children, I felt quite superior to women who were stay-at-home mothers. I often thought that they were a bit like proud, contented cows who were not capable of doing anything more challenging. I, in contrast, was doing really important work. I even remember, much to my own embarrassment, that my first reaction to Betty Friedan's *The Feminine Mystique* was: "That book is going to make trouble. It's going to make women unmanageable. Who will tend to the children and the homes if they all decide that they want to go out and *fulfill* [said sarcastically] themselves?" Of course, I was going to work, but I was an exception, or so I thought. For the ordinary woman, her place was basically in the home tending to others.

Now I see these attitudes as an indication of a very well-developed Inner Patriarch who was playing a major role in my life at that time, a role that I knew nothing about. My Inner Patriarch ruled my behavior in my marriage and in my career. He kept me "appropriately" deferent to the men in my life and limited my power in the world. He encouraged me to distrust women and to trust only men. He discouraged me from any behaviors that he saw as weak, irrational, and feminine. My femininity was appropriate only when it would please the men in my life.

As I learned about my Inner Patriarch—and from him—I was able to change the ways in which he influenced me. This was particularly helpful in two areas: (1) my intimate relationships with men, and (2) my power in the world. I could see that many of my Inner Patriarch's values were quite admirable, and that he knew a great deal about the world, particularly the world of men. He knew what was acceptable and what was not. He also knew how I could keep my traditionally feminine qualities even while I developed power.

The changes were very gratifying. My relationship with my husband, which had been good, became even richer, more objective, and more equal. We were truly partners. Actually, this was why I was comfortable changing my last name to his after 14 year of marriage. The change in name felt like an affirmation of partnership; it no longer felt as if I were becoming an appendage or a possession with no independent identity of my own.

As for power, I became comfortable bringing more of my feminine energy into the world. Before this, my power was limited to that which the Inner Patriarch found acceptable, the power of the mind. In the past, I had tried to emulate men and, because I was a woman, I could only be an imitation man. As my Inner Patriarch changed, I became a woman of feminine power. I was able to bring forth my own power and my own way of being in the world that was different from traditionally male power.

### Making Changes

*There is much of value in the patriarchal beliefs and rules that are carried by our Inner Patriarchs; we must be cautious and respectful as we make our changes. We can accept the gifts that the Shadow King offers and decline the humiliations and limitations that he might wish to impose upon us. We can keep what works for us and transform whatever seems too restrictive.* We can restore the dignity and power of the masculine/feminine balance within ourselves. We can make choices about what we do rather than react automatically to unknown forces. As the belief system of the Inner Patriarch changes, his ability to hold his ground in the face of adversity can be a great asset to each of us.

In order to make these changes, we must first learn about our Inner Patriarch. Where does he come from? What does he sound like? What impact does he have on our lives? You will hear him and learn about his beliefs, his rules, and his values. *We will bring him out of the shadows so that he is no longer a Shadow King. Once we do this, you will have direct access to him. You will make what was unconscious, conscious. At this point, real change is possible.*

### Voice Dialogue and the Psychology of Selves

Let me begin by briefly introducing you to the basic tools I have used in my studies of this Shadow King. We humans are not as simple as we sometimes think. Our psyches are made up of many parts. Some of these parts we know about, and others are hidden in the unconscious. We are all proud of some parts of ourselves and ashamed of others. My husband, Hal Stone, and I are both psychologists, and we have spent the past 24 years studying these "parts" of the human psyche which we call "selves." Others have called them "voices" or "subpersonalities" or "the many I's." All of us are made up of selves. We call the study of these selves and their roles in our lives "the Psychology of Selves." My work with the Inner Patriarch is an outgrowth of our joint work with these selves. Since it is built upon the foundation that Hal and I established together, I would like to give you a brief description of our work.*

Initially, it was quite a surprise for us to discover these selves, to learn that they were quite real, and to see how they operated in people's lives (including our own, of course). Over the years, they have been a source of unending fascination! We have found that each self is unique; each has its own look, its own history, its own values, and its own areas of expertise. For us, there are no good selves and no bad selves.

Each self has its good points and its bad points. For instance, I have a self that I call my Pusher. She wants me to get things done. She wants me to write this book. It was my Pusher that just dragged me out of my delicious hammock on this beautiful spring day and sat me down at my computer. I can guarantee that without my Pusher I would get nothing done! At a moment like this, I really need her to pull me away from the distractions that surround me. But she can push me unmercifully, even when this is totally inappropriate. She can make me feel that I should be working even when this is not necessary. She is unable to tolerate relaxation or just "being." She is definitely a "doing" self.

Our lives are dominated by the selves we call "primary selves." These are the selves that determine who we are and what we do. They are who we think we are. One of my primary selves has been my Pusher. On the opposite side we have what we call our "disowned selves," the ones that we have discarded or repressed. In this case, the disowned self would be my Beach Bum. The primary

---

* More complete information is available in our books *Embracing Our Selves* and *Embracing Each Other*.

selves judge and fear these disowned selves. My Pusher fears my Beach Bum; she fears that if I allow myself to relax for too long, I will forget how to work and that I will become useless. Being a useless person is totally unacceptable to the Pushers of the world.

Now if my Pusher is my primary self and I do not have access to my Beach Bum or my Party Girl, I will work all through my vacation. My Pusher is the kind of self that would bring along all the boring unread journal articles when I take a trip to a tropic isle because, to her way of thinking, I have nothing else to do on the island, and I would finally have the free time to read them. She would be proud of herself for her great efficiency. She would not think about the fact that my husband might want a bit of attention or that I could use a little romance. Incidentally, with the wonderful new electronic offices, we are never far from an office and we can read, write, fax, e-mail, and phone from anywhere to anywhere in the world. This is truly heaven for the Pushers of the world, mine included.

If I do not know about these selves, I have no choices in life. I behave automatically. My Pusher will run my life, and I will be uneasy whenever I have nothing to do. All of us can learn about these selves, separate from them, and have choice about which self appears in our lives at which time. I do not want my Beach Bum around when it is time to write, and I do not want my Pusher around when it is time for romance.

How did we learn about these selves? Through a simple and amazingly effective tool that we discovered, a method we call "Voice Dialogue." We just talk directly to the selves. Let us take the example of my Pusher. If I want to find out about my Pusher, I would simply ask someone to interview her. We call this interviewer the "facilitator." I am "the subject." The Pusher is the self being interviewed. We have found that the selves are more than happy to talk.

What does a Voice Dialogue session look like? The facilitator asks me (the subject) to move over to where my Pusher is, and I move to another place in the room. I could move my chair, sit in another chair, sit on the floor, stand, whatever feels appropriate. My Pusher does not sit in the same place that I do. This helps to separate her from me. Then the facilitator talks to my Pusher and asks her about herself. If the facilitator knows about selves, and shows genuine respect and interest, the self responds freely. In this case, my Pusher will tell the facilitator with great pride: "I have gotten a great deal accomplished. I am responsible for the degrees, the books, and the efficiency of her child-rearing. I have never wasted time, opportunities, or money. I am extremely good at what I do."

It was in this way, using Voice Dialogue, that Hal and I learned about the many selves and the ways in which they affect people's behavior. Most of the material in this book was collected during Voice Dialogue sessions. I have included both longer segments of sessions and short quotations.

Dreams are another important way to find out about these selves. The characters in our dreams represent our different selves. We can use dreams to discover these selves and to learn about how they are operating in our lives. For instance, I am interviewed on the radio, and I am authoritative, outgoing, and powerful. My Inner Patriarch is unhappy with my behavior, which he sees as unfeminine, but I do not know about this. That night when I go to sleep, I dream that I am being put into prison by an authoritarian, rational, cold man (my Inner Patriarch) because I did not obey the rules. Thus, my dreams give me a clear, objective, and memorable picture of what is happening in the shadows beyond my everyday consciousness. That is why I have used dreams, my own and others', to illustrate many aspects of the Inner Patriarch.

This introduction has given you the frame of reference within which the work on the Inner Patriarch developed. Now that the stage is set, let us begin the drama of the Shadow King.

# INTRODUCING
# THE INNER PATRIARCH

# CHAPTER ONE

# THE REALM OF THE SHADOW KING

*There were no demands from the outside, so it
must have been something within each woman
responsible for this loss of herself. Something
was operating unconsciously, in the shadows.*

The air felt almost liquid as everyone leaned forward, riveted by the tale that Lucille was telling. The women's group had been meeting for over an hour, and the sharing of life experiences had gradually gotten deeper and deeper. It was as though each woman brought forth photos of particularly meaningful milestones in her life and then told about them, free to talk about these experiences because there were only women present. There was seriousness, but there was much laughter as well.

The women spoke about birth, life, and death. The sense of awe deepened. Now Lucille was describing an abortion that had begun as an ordinary impersonal hospital procedure, but had ended with her lying in a bed in a pool of blood with the aborted fetus. It seemed as though the staff had deliberately left her alone; nobody responded to her calls for assistance. Everyone in the group sat in stunned silence, supporting Lucille and empathizing with her pain, isolation, and terror. Each woman had her own story of past abortions, each pictured herself in Lucille's situation.

The group felt like a single organism, breathing in unison. The women began to talk again, this time in hushed and reverent tones. It felt almost holy. Suddenly, off in another part of the building, there were sounds of shouts and laughter. The men's group was obviously disbanding. The response of the women was astounding. In an instant, they dropped what they had been doing as though it was totally meaningless. What had been a single organism was now a group of individual women, each one listening for the sound of her own man's voice. The sense of awe had vanished, and their power was completely gone.

What had happened to them? Who had so totally distracted them from themselves? There were no demands from the outside, so it must have been something within each woman responsible for this loss of herself. Something, or someone, was operating unconsciously, ruling from the shadows. I had no name for who that was or what had happened, but the experience stayed with me. I knew that I had caught a glimpse of something important, but I did not know what it was. So I waited and I watched, wondering if something similar would occur, and it did.

Several months later, I was in Holland. As I sat in a group of women, I began to feel uncomfortable. They were, for the most part, women that I knew, but as I looked around at them I felt as though I was surrounded by a group of judgmental, humorless male strangers, a group of patriarchs who had no use for women or women's groups. I realized that whatever was happening was related to the sudden loss of self that I had witnessed in the past. I asked about this and, sure enough, the women were thinking that a group of women could never do anything important and that they would prefer to be with the men. Fortunately, I had thought a great deal about this issue, and I did not take their rejection of me personally. Since I was truly curious, and this was a Voice Dialogue workshop, I asked if I might speak to the self that felt this way about women. A number of women volunteered.

A young, talented, and very intelligent Dutch woman named Mara volunteered to let me talk to the part of her, the self, that thought so little of women. It was an amazing experience for both of us! Mara was beautiful, charming, and very feminine. Mara's

Inner Patriarch was not. He was masculine, extremely powerful, humorless, and judgmental. He was her Shadow King, the Inner Patriarch who operated in the shadows of her unconscious and determined much of her behavior. My search was over; this was the mysterious voice I had been looking for.

When Mara's Inner Patriarch spoke, he was stern and compelling; you could almost see his long, flowing biblical robes. His authority commanded respect. It would be impossible to ignore him. His views were his views, and there was no way to change him, to placate him, or reason with him. He was absolutely sure that he knew exactly what the world was like and how it should be run. This meant that it should be run by men and that women should accept their naturally inferior status.

This Inner Patriarch was different from the Inner Critic, a self that I had met many times before. I feel that it is important for you to see the distinction between these two selves. The Inner Critic is the critical voice within each of us that comments constantly upon who we are and what we do. However, the Inner Critic does not care whether you are a man or a woman. It just likes to criticize; that is its job in life. The Inner Critic is a much more individualized and personal voice than the Inner Patriarch and it, too, has a great impact upon our lives.*

In contrast to the Inner Critic, this Inner Patriarch cared very much about Mara's gender. He had totally different expectations, opinions, and standards for men and for women. These were independent of Mara and his specific feelings about her. In general, the Inner Patriarch expected nothing good from Mara or, for that matter, from any other woman, just because they were women. His basic attitude was that women were inferior to men, and nothing they might do could change that immutable fact.

The Inner Critic, in contrast, usually gives the impression that we are personally responsible for whatever is "wrong" with us and

---

* If you want to find out more about the Inner Critic, read *Embracing Your Inner Critic* by Hal Stone and myself.

that if we were to work hard enough, even if we are women, success just might be possible. For example, Shelly has just written a long report for her department. Her Inner Critic picks it apart, showing her all the ways that it could be better. Even after she has corrected these, her Inner Critic lets her know that there is more to be done. Then it points out that her report is not as good as Alicia's. Shelly continues her revisions until she can do no more. Actually, the report is quite good. But her Inner Critic tells her that although it is now better than Alicia's, it is not as good as the first set of reports that Shelly herself had written earlier in her career, the ones that won her the promotion to department chief. Her Inner Critic is never satisfied, but keeps urging her on with the implicit assumption that she can succeed if only she tries harder. In contrast, her Inner Patriarch looks at the report and lets her know that it is good enough for a woman. In his eyes, nothing she can do will ever make Shelly's work as good or important as a man's.

### The Subversion of Women's Power

As I listened to Mara's Inner Patriarch, I could hear that he was the inner spokesman for the outer patriarchy. I realized that he had a great impact upon the way we women viewed ourselves and our role in the world. He divided humankind into women and men and saw these two groups as basically different. Each group had its own territory or arena of power and its own gifts to bring to the world. The gifts of the men were important, and the gifts of the women were secondary. Traditionally, male power was supported, and female power was subverted.

I could see that this had two practical consequences. First, the Inner Patriarch defines us as women, telling us what real woman are like and defining our capabilities and limitations. Secondly, he trivializes whatever it is that women are and what they do. Thus, he undervalues the portions of the world that belong to the traditionally feminine. These are undervalued in men as well as women. We, as human beings, learn that half of the gifts that we bring into this world, that is, the gifts that have customarily been associated with the feminine, are not important or really valuable. Since this has great cultural impact, let us think about these gifts.

## The Gifts

*I dream that I must appear before a judge. He looks dependable, responsible, and authoritative. I am carrying a wrapped package, which contains something both precious and powerful; it feels as though it is the gift of my deepest female nature. I have worked hard to package this gift properly. I have left an air space around the contents so that they will not get crushed, and I must guard the entire package carefully so that it will not collapse. I am also carrying a very carefully polished brass candlestick with a candle in it.*

*My dilemma is as follows: Am I going to deliver my package and allow someone else to open it and to use the contents, or am I going to light my candle and sing my own song? I would feel safe turning over the unopened package to this judge, because then I would not be responsible for its contents. But if I do so, he will be in charge of the contents, and I will forfeit the right to light my own candle and to sing my own song.*

That judge is my Inner Patriarch, and this dream gives me a clear picture of my dilemma as a woman. If I give my package to my Inner Patriarch, then he will judge its contents and take charge of my life. I will be considered inferior to men, but I will be safe, blameless, and protected. If I follow his orders, I will not get into trouble. If I keep my own package, then I keep my power and my individuality, but these gifts will be my responsibility.

What are the specifically female gifts and the basic sources of power that are in this package? I have considered this question as a woman, a daughter, a mother of daughters, and a psychologist. I see these gifts as the power of a woman's sexuality, her ability to attract others, the intensity of her need for relationship, her

5

capacity to support and to care for others, her intuition, her natural connection to her emotions and, of course, her childbearing capability. But the voice within each of us, the Inner Patriarch that has its roots deep within the patriarchal culture that has nourished and protected us, deprives us of the right to enjoy these gifts. At best, it trivializes them; at worst, it shames us for possessing them.

We are not taught how to honor and develop these traditionally feminine gifts as true sources of power; they are devalued. We are also not shown how to include the aspects of ourselves that are more traditionally masculine in nature in our overall development. As girls growing into womanhood, we have had few, if any, popular myths or mature heroines to guide us. We have almost no examples of women who have developed both their feminine nature and their power. In our culture, there is a split between what is female and what is powerful. When we see a woman who is beautiful, loving, and sensual, we automatically assume that she does not have great wisdom or power. The opposite is also true; we rarely think of a woman of wisdom and power as loving and sensual (even if she should happen to be).

There also seems to be a separation between motherhood and power. There is not a similar split between fatherhood and power. There are many tales of wise, benevolent, handsome, and powerful kings, or even gods, who are also fathers, but never a story of a mature woman, a benevolent, wise, sensual, beautiful, and powerful queen, who is also a mother. Queens, particularly those who are mothers, are more often obstructions or problems than great leaders. The "evil queen" is almost as common an image as the "good king."

This is not true everywhere on our planet. In some older indigenous cultures, there is respect for the natural power of women. She can be a true woman and still have power. Carolyn Conger, one of our American wise women, told me of her contacts with the Maoris, the indigenous peoples of New Zealand. When she visited there, a group of leading Maori healers was brought together to meet her as a respected member of the international healing community.

Before she entered the gathering, Carolyn was asked never to step over a man's legs if he was sitting on the ground. The reason for this was that the power in her vagina was so intense that it would automatically suck the power out of the men. And all during the meetings, their chief shaman could never look directly into her eyes. He was able to see the power that she carried and feared that she might take something away from him.

I am not advocating that we move into a position of having this kind of unequal power or that we adopt the belief systems of the Maoris, but I do think that there is something important for us to learn from them. Let us now consider the unique gifts that we as women have traditionally offered to our species, the gifts that at this moment are still subject to the evaluation and the control of our Inner Patriarchs.

### The Gifts of Life, of Relationship, and of Caring for Others

Fundamentally, women are responsible for the continuity of human life on this planet. They are needed to create life. They are also capable of destroying it. If women no longer chose to have children, if they chose not to nurture the children that they did have and allowed them to die, or if they actually killed their offspring, there would no longer be human life (as we know it) on this planet. This is a fact that has long been overlooked by the dominant patriarchal culture. It is also overlooked by the Inner Patriarch, who sees women as basically helpless and without any natural power in the world.

In our awesome scientific zeal, we humans have moved far enough to make the creation of life possible without the presence of a live man. We can choose to breed the most genetically perfect beings should we care to do so. But we have not yet found a way to adequately replace a live woman in the prenatal nourishment

and development of a human fetus, or a way to replace the nourishment provided by relationship and a parent's love after birth.

Loving, nurturing human contact is urgently needed after the
birth of a child so that it will thrive and grow up whole. If this is
not provided, we bring up damaged, unsocialized humans who, at
best, are personally unhappy and, at worst, are a danger to others.
This ability to nurture others, to care deeply for them, and to put
their emotional and physical needs before one's own has been seen
as a basically feminine or female quality in our culture. Since the
Inner Patriarch sees this as womanly and natural, it is, of course,
unimportant. He would never think of rewarding mothers for a job
well done in the same way that he would think of rewarding someone who works in the marketplace. For him, the idea of a mother
expecting a bonus because she has done a good job at home is un-
thinkable, but he would certainly give the same woman a bonus
if she produced a new product or a new source of income for her
company at work.

The complexities of running a household and truly attending to
the needs of children are only now beginning to be appreciated by
the outer world, but again the Inner Patriarch lags behind. My own
Inner Patriarch was totally unimpressed by childrearing even when
I became a mother and he could see what mothering entailed. He
never did give me much credit for childrearing and always saw it
as a bit of a vacation from "real life." He admitted that I was behaving like a good, responsible, thoughtful mother at home, but
he truly admired me only during the hours I was professionally
active.

It was a particular experience at work that caused me to separate from my Inner Patriarch and to question his values for the first
time. I had become the executive director of a residential treatment center for adolescent girls, a very challenging position. I was
responsible for a staff of about 35, the finances of the institution
(both raising the necessary funds and spending them wisely), the
building, the program, and the care of a group of acting-out

adolescent girls for whom we provided residence, an on-grounds school, 24-hour-a-day supervision, and therapy. I was often asked how I kept track of everything, and my heartfelt response was: "This is a very demanding and exciting job, but it is much easier than staying at home full time and raising three children! Not only that, but here I have an excellent support staff to share the work, I get paid, and I get lots of recognition for what I do." I knew this from personal experience, and my Inner Patriarch could not convince me otherwise.

Thus, we can see some of the ways in which the Inner Patriarch echoes the values of the outer patriarchy and affects the way that we, as women, view our gifts. It has not always been this way. Before the destruction of the matriarchal societies and the development of our patriarchal system, things were different. In the ancient matriarchal, agrarian societies many, or most, of the deities were female, and the Great Mother was worshiped as the Supreme Deity. There were priestesses as well as priests. Not only did the religion honor the female, but the legal system did as well. Both lineage and laws of inheritance were traced through the mother, and there was at least equal, if not dominant, political, religious, and economic power held by women. Our patriarchal system reversed this situation approximately 6,000 years ago. This change brought new gifts of its own, but it devalued what came before. Let us see what happened to change our perceptions of these gifts.

### The Gift Is Turned into a Curse

> "I will greatly multiply thy sorrow and thy conception; in sorrow thou shalt bring forth children; and thy desire shall be to thy husband and he shall rule over thee."
>
> — Genesis

So it is that we as women find our unique gifts cursed in the very first chapter of the Bible. The very gifts that we carry—the gifts of bringing forth life, cherishing and sustaining life, and the deep-seated longing for relationship—have been turned into a burden and have become the curse of the women who carry them. As we look at what has happened to these gifts, we enter the realm of the Shadow King.

Until recently, relationship, marriage and childbearing were essentially a woman's only choice in our patriarchal society, and the Shadow King still agrees with this point of view. This was a woman's job in the world, whether or not she liked it. But relationship was no longer viewed as a gift; it had been turned into an anxiety-filled curse. The average woman worried that she would not have a proper place in ordinary society if she did not have a proper husband. Most women, and their Inner Patriarchs as well, viewed marriage and childbearing as their primary goal in life. They devoted the greater part of their early lives to "catching" a good husband. For the women who valued their freedom and independence, this requirement to be married and bear children was not very attractive.

Times have changed, and now we have moved over to the opposite point of view. In our current social and political climate, the woman who longs for a monogamous primary relationship—in the past, we called this "a marriage"—often feels uncomfortable. She wonders if she is lacking something within herself when she feels a need for someone else to share her life. This attitude is an indication that the Inner Patriarch is working in the shadows of the unconscious. There is a "Catch-22," however. Although he still requires a "real" woman to be married, the Inner Patriarch basically sees the yearning for relationship as womanly and, therefore, evidence of weakness. He has no idea that this need for relationship, the desire to be partnered, might be a gift.

I have spoken to many intelligent and competent women in their thirties and forties who feel ashamed and weak because they are actively seeking a husband. They are uncomfortable because their Inner Patriarchs judge this quest as a sign of inferiority, and the goal of marriage as a womanly pursuit rather than a manly one. These women are embarrassed to let others know that they want to get married and that they are looking for a husband. Their friends or families usually worry about them and see this search as a real problem or, at best, a serious challenge.

It is a rare woman who allows herself to see this search for a husband as a proper age-appropriate goal and goes forth to attain this goal in an organized, businesslike fashion using all the resources at her command. Instead, most women put their trust in luck and, at best, make sporadic, disorganized, and unfocused attempts to meet someone. They certainly would not treat a professional or work-related goal in this way!

Interestingly enough, when a man in his thirties or forties decides that it's time to get married, the announcement that he is looking for a wife is usually greeted with joy, as though he has made a mature decision and is now ready to settle down. His friends and family are delighted to help him, and are usually confident that sooner or later he will meet someone appropriate. There is an expectation that it will take some time and several attempts, but this is not a deterrent. Thus, the same decision is seen as a sign of maturity and manliness in a male, and as a sign of weakness and neediness in a woman. This discrepancy is always an indication of the Inner Patriarch at work.

Let us look at how the traditionally feminine gift of caring for others has been turned into a curse, first by the outer patriarchy and now by the Inner Patriarch. On the one hand, this natural need for relationship in women has always been valued. Until very recently, women were encouraged to approach the world as loving and responsible caregivers. On the other hand, this same need to care for others was seen as a weakness and was often used as a means of manipulation, exploitation, and domination. Women were expected to do this because this was their nature. Therefore, they should not require anything in return for the gift of love and nurturing that they bestowed upon others. The Inner Patriarch still carries these values, and we can see the cultural result: women expect to be caregivers, and they are often exploited as such.

In fulfilling this role of the caregiver and the protector of relationship and family, women have learned to move beyond their own needs in order to meet the needs of others. This has been creative and quite wonderful in many ways, but women have paid a high price. We have lost our ability to make choices, to know what it is that we want, and to think for ourselves. It feels as though, in the realm of the Shadow King, there is a law that says: "Others come first." Women can only do as they wish after everyone else has been cared for.

However, it is the women who have disobeyed this law and who have moved away from these distinctively female gifts of relating and caretaking who are most likely to meet with outer success. They are more likely to receive recognition in the world and financial rewards than the women who have devoted their lives to family, lovers, and friends. Thus, the women who have disowned the traditional roles that emphasize relationship and nurturing are more likely to be valued by the Inner Patriarch. They are the ones seen as having led productive, fulfilling, and successful lives.

Success and productivity do not usually equate to what we might think of as the ultimate act of creativity—the bringing forth of new life. Instead, in the realm of the Shadow King, this ability to bring forth new life has been, until recent years, like a jail sentence that a woman was forced to complete whether or not she wished to do so. It was her duty to get pregnant and then to finish the pregnancy. This is the belief of the Shadow King, even though the woman may not have desired a child in the first place, and a new child might well create an unlivable situation.

To do otherwise, to terminate an unwanted pregnancy, has been viewed as a sin and, in previous decades, has been written into our laws as illegal. In the interests of protecting the new life of the fetus, the woman's choice in this matter, her own needs, and her own life have been overlooked. It is my feeling that her awesome—yes, truly awesome—ability to create and destroy life is something that has felt dangerous to her, something that the patriarchal society has needed to control. The knowledge that this is true power is something that the Inner Patriarch denies to women.

For me, the fear of this power over life and death is the underlying issue in the battle over abortion. Yes, abortion is killing an unborn child. The taking of life is a sin. It is an action to be considered very, very carefully. But most women are uncomfortable saying this aloud and then standing behind their actions when they do have an abortion. The carefully considered decision of a woman to kill is too threatening, too evil in this realm of the Shadow King.

I find it interesting that this moral issue is never considered when, as a nation, we decide to go to war. There, too, lives are taken—many lives, in fact. But I have never heard heated discussions over the rights of the people we are planning to kill when we go to war, only concern about our own projected casualties. And now with the automatic use of air power, we are not killing just the warriors who have chosen to go to war, but we are also killing innocent noncombatants as well. I am not talking only about the outer world of policy makers or of men when I speak of this contrast in value judgments, but of our Inner Patriarchs, too. War, even in the Bible, is seen as an act of power if you do it for the right reason, but abortion, a woman's ultimate act of power (if we admit that it involves killing) is always seen as a sin.

### Aphrodite's Gifts of Sexuality and Attraction

Aphrodite's gifts of sensual enjoyment, beauty, relationship, and the ability to attract and to connect with others are precious. There are few sights as totally seductive and charming as a little girl who is beginning to feel this power. She shamelessly flirts, she primps, she caresses others, and she enjoys her power to attract. Others love to be with her. Mothers love to feel her combing their hair, fathers love to feel her cuddling up in their laps. She makes everyone around her feel good. Similarly, a grown woman's sensuality and her sexual nature can be breathtaking. Her ability to attract is immense.

In the realm of the Shadow King, these gifts are always associated with femininity and often viewed with distrust. Wouldn't it be interesting if our world were to value attraction more, and if men, as well as women, were permitted to enjoy their Aphrodite nature? What if we, as Brianne Swimme suggests in *The Universe Is a Green Dragon*, paid more attention to what attracts us? What if we valued attraction and what holds us together instead of concentrating upon our differences and what holds us apart? I would suggest that the world might be quite different. Gravity, or the law of attraction, seems to work pretty well in the physical world.

This reminds me of an apocryphal story about an area up here in Northern California. This part of the country was settled by Russian seal traders. That is why we have a Russian River and there are towns with names such as Sebastopol. Well, there came a time when this began to be a problem. The Mexicans held territory as far north as San Francisco, and they were not too happy having the Russians so close by. Now, if everyone had concentrated upon differences, there would have been a war to settle matters. But, instead, Aphrodite came to the rescue. It seems as though the daughter of the governor of San Francisco and the commanding officer at Ft. Ross (the Russians' headquarters) fell in love. This led to some very pleasant negotiations, and matters were settled easily. The fort and the Russian holdings were sold to Mexico, and all was peacefully settled.

In the realm of the Shadow King, however, attraction is to be used, not enjoyed. Women have been taught to be ashamed of their Aphrodite nature. Sensuality has been equated with sexuality, and both have been demeaned. A woman's sexuality has been turned into a commodity. It is used to sell products, movies, or even the women themselves. According to the laws of this kingdom, sensuality and sexuality are to be controlled and ruled over by men and never to be enjoyed for their own sake by women. If a woman claims the right to these pleasures, she has gone against timeless rules, and her Inner Patriarch will be mighty upset!

So, we see that these traditionally feminine gifts have been turning sour, which results in serious consequences. As these gifts have been trivialized, not only women, but men, too, have been discouraged from enjoying them. As such, men have suffered this loss equally with women, and many of the delights of being human have been denied to them as well. If they cared deeply about relationships, love, and sensuality, and if they wanted to participate in childrearing, they would be admitting that they felt as women did, and this, according to the beliefs of the Shadow King, would be admitting their inferiority. Let us now meet the one who carries these beliefs, our Shadow King, the Inner Patriarch.

# THE INNER PATRIARCH

*I dream that I am climbing a pyramid that I have been climbing for some time. I am exhausted, and the closer I get to the top, the more tired I become. I carry with me important information that I have gathered and sorted through over these past years. It is in a file folder and very well organized.*

*As I begin to climb the last terrace [or set of steps], there is a man standing at the base of the pyramid who urges me to stop. He tells me that it requires too much effort and that this will do harm to me. He suggests that I stop here and let some man take my portfolio the remainder of the way to the top.*

*As I listen to him, I know that he does, indeed, care about me and that he has my best interests at heart. He fears that I cannot push my way up this last ascent, and he feels that a man could climb it easily. He wants to spare me the trouble of too much exertion.*

*I realize that by listening to this man in the past, I have become weak and have lost the ability to stretch myself to the limit. I see that I no longer try to push just a little bit harder in order to keep moving beyond my earlier limitations. I then take my portfolio with me and, by myself, I climb the last set of steps to reach the top. I am exhausted, but delighted that I have pushed through and moved up another level.*

*I feel that this move is very important. Not only have I reached the next level, but I have broken an old, old habit of*

17

*listening to this man's opinions of my strength and allowing him
to define my limitations.*

We women are like the woman in my dream. We have important information and experiences to contribute to the world, and we are trying to take the next step forward. For a while, it seemed as if we were going to be able to do this easily. But, as long as the Shadow King continues to hold us back, he and his laws make this climb very tiring.

*The ancient patriarchal traditions that are represented by the man in
this dream [my own Inner Patriarch] lie deep within the unconscious of
each of us. Since he is unconscious, he rules us from the shadows, and
we may not notice him except when he materializes in our dreams.* He is capable of distracting us from our tasks and taking from us the portfolios that carry our knowledge and experience. If we resist him, this resistance can tire us so that we do not have the energy we need to finish our movement to the next level.

### What Is the Inner Patriarch?

*The Inner Patriarch is the voice, or subpersonality, within us that carries the ancient patriarchal traditions, values, and rules of the last six millennia. Like the men in the dream, he is an internalized version of the outer patriarchy. As with the outer patriarchy, he functions both protectively and destructively.*

In his positive aspect, the Inner Patriarch, much like the outer patriarchy, supports women and helps to make them feel safe. He feels protective of us and is intent on keeping us safely confined within old, well-defined boundaries so that we will not be exposed to danger or disappointment. In this positive aspect, he supports us and helps to make us safe in our roles as mothers and daughters. He watches over us with concern whenever we venture out into the world of men.

In his negative aspect, the Inner Patriarch, again mirroring the outer patriarchy, sees women as generally inferior to men. He does not think that we, as women, are capable of caring for ourselves without the protection and help of a man. Although his intentions are praiseworthy when he offers us assistance (again, like the men in the dream), he does not trust a woman to achieve anything important alone. *When we accept the Inner Patriarch's assessment of our abilities, we become weakened. Conversely, when we fight against his views, when we insist that we will never allow a man to help us and that we must do everything alone or with other women, we continue to allow our Inner Patriarchs to define our reality and to interfere with our creativity. We do not have the option to interact comfortably with men as equal and caring human beings.*

As women have noticed, particularly over the past 30 years, there are also truly destructive aspects of the outer patriarchy. These include the exploitation, domination, and devaluation of women. We women have struggled to change this outer patriarchy for about a generation now and have been amazingly successful in modifying its power in many areas. In my own lifetime, I have seen women gain more control over their own bodies, minds, and destinies than was ever imagined in the past. In all fairness, though, I must point out that it was the women who had been protected and nourished by these self-same patriarchal values of our culture who were able to accomplish this!

*But as difficult as it has been to fight an enemy outside, at least it was visible and obviously a threat. It is the unseen enemy that is currently a problem.* When we are not aware of the voice within us that echoes the opinions, judgments, and values of the outer patriarchy, we cannot deal with it effectively. The Inner Patriarch operates in the shadows of our unconscious and affects our thoughts, feelings, and actions from within.

Underneath it all, the Inner Patriarch fears that we will not be able to succeed in what he still sees as a man's world. For most of us, he has his doubts about women. He either questions our intelligence, knowledge, and abilities, or is concerned about our emotionality, our trustworthiness, our self-discipline, and our power. It is amazing to discover his existence within us, to hear his voice, and to see the areas he continues to dominate. Although this Inner Patriarch operates in men as well as women, I will concentrate upon his role in the psyche of women, touching only briefly upon his role in the psyche of men.

### The Inner Patriarch As One of Our Many Selves

This Inner Patriarch is only one of the many selves (or sub-personalities) that live within us. These selves are the building blocks of our psyches, and they carry all the energies known to humankind, both the admired and the despised. The selves that make up our persona and determine who we are in the world, are our "primary selves." These develop early in life to protect our vulnerability, to help us avoid pain, and to enable us to adapt to the world around us. The type of primary self that we develop will depend upon many factors. These include genetic, emotional, and spiritual predispositions. They also include environmental factors, such as the psychological dynamics of the family of origin, birth order, ethnic background, gender, religious affiliation, schools attended, physical location, nationality and time in history.

Rhonda, for instance, was the oldest daughter of a well-to-do but dysfunctional mother whose husband divorced her when Rhonda was still quite young. Early in life, Rhonda saw that if she did not take care of herself, her mother, and her younger siblings, nobody's emotional needs would ever be met. Therefore, she developed a primary self that we could call a Responsible Mother. This Responsible Mother was strong, self-reliant, responsible, and sensible. She took care of other people, putting their needs and sensitivities before her own. In this way, she indirectly took care of Rhonda's feelings and sensitivities by creating a safe and comfortable environment for her and for those around her.

Sally, on the other hand, had a very efficient, rational, controlling mother and father. Her home was well run, and all her physical needs were met. However, Sally felt that there was something missing. She felt that her parents' life lacked meaning and spirit, and she yearned for more. She was an introverted and sensitive child, the third in the family. The older children were achievement-oriented like their parents, but Sally was different. She began her spiritual search early, drawn to the picture of a better world. Sally felt that her purpose was to help build this world and this mission gave a meaning, richness, and depth to her life that was lacking in her parents'. Thus, Sally's primary self was her Spiritual Self.

For every primary self, there is an equal and opposite self or set of selves. We call these the "disowned selves." In order for Rhonda to function primarily from her Responsible Mother, she had to disown the opposing selves, the ones that would keep her from taking care of others. This meant that Rhonda would disown the selves in her that would think about her own needs, selves that could be dependent upon others or receive from them. Rhonda would also disown the part of her that could be more relaxed and not forced to do everything perfectly. Sally, in turn, would disown the selves that could take pleasure in the material world and would allow her to be self-indulgent. She would also disown the parts that could take pleasure in "meaningless" activities such as watching TV or shopping.

Although the Inner Patriarch is a self that usually operates behind the scenes, he has a great deal of power and is, in his way, a primary self. He is one of our inner lawmakers and carries with him a set of rules, values, and expectations that are extremely influential. As I have said, the primary selves are influenced by our personal environment. The Inner Patriarch is influenced by a larger environment, by our civilization, and the era that is just drawing to an end. We can think of him as the voice of our culture. *Although the culture around us has been changing during the past 30 years, for most of us the Inner Patriarch still sounds like an old-fashioned father who dwells within us; we women remain children to his opinions, his rules, and his expectations.* Interestingly enough, the information that he carries has most often been passed on to us by our mothers and not by our fathers.

### What Are the Values of the Inner Patriarch?

The Inner Patriarch is concerned with law and order. He has a great deal to say on the subject of women and clearly defined gender roles. He feels that men should be men, in the traditional sense of manliness, and women should be traditionally feminine. He has no respect for a man who carries feminine attributes nor for a woman who carries masculine attributes. The "Catch-22" in this system is as follows: (1) women should be womanly; (2) if they are not womanly, they are failures as women; (3) if they are womanly, they are inferior to men because traditional feminine qualities are inferior to traditionally masculine qualities.

What does the Inner Patriarch expect of women? The Inner Patriarch thinks that a good woman should be supportive, receptive, loving, giving, compassionate, understanding, and nurturing. She should not be too powerful, and she should not take up too much space. He likes his women submissive and tame. He fears what will happen to the world—and to the women themselves—if women were to stand up and take power either in the outer world or in the more personal world of relationship.

The Inner Patriarch truly worries that women, if they learn about their own inclinations and desires and become self-indulgent, will seriously upset the world in which we all live. As far as men are concerned, the Inner Patriarch feels that it is important for them to remain strong and in control. Men must protect civilization as we know it through strength and discipline. Men and women are different, and they should remain different.

## What Are the Inner Patriarch's Primary Concerns?

There are four primary topics about which the Inner Patriarch has particularly strong feelings. These are relationship, power, sexuality, and emotionality/self-control. However, he does not necessarily emphasize the same areas of concern in all women.

For some women, his concern focuses upon only one or two of these areas. For most women, his voice can still be heard commenting about all four. There are women who have quieted their Inner Patriarchs in one or another of these areas by one of the following life styles: (1) They have dealt directly with the outer patriarchy and have been successful and powerful in the world of men. (2) They have led more traditionally feminine lives as wives and mothers. (3) They have led spiritual lives that removed them from the challenges of sexuality and power in the world of men.

Many women in this first category who have concentrated their efforts upon dealing with the outer patriarchy have been quite successful. Their Inner Patriarchs no longer worry about their ability to achieve power and success in a man's world, but they remain very concerned about relationship. They make comments such as: "Sure she has succeeded in business, but I don't think she's a real woman. You'll see, she'll never find a man." The patriarch often then moves on to the next comment, "She's not a real woman. Anyone who acts the way she does is more of a man than a woman."

There are some women who have succeeded in freeing themselves totally from their Inner Patriarch's concerns about both their power and their sexuality by safely and successfully managing their activities in both areas. Nonetheless, it is quite common for the Inner Patriarch's voice to emerge once again when these women become involved in a committed relationship or when they get married. The power that these women feel at work or in the world dissolves when they come home and walk through the door. They are tigers at work and children at home. This striking change is due, at least in part, to the Inner Patriarch's rules about the woman's role in relationship.

### What Does the Inner Patriarch Sound Like?

I have spoken to many Inner Patriarchs over the years. Even though they might have our best interests at heart, for the most part, they speak very negatively about women. It can be useful to look at a sampling of the kinds of statements they make. As you read through this list, note which ones sound familiar to you. Perhaps only one or two will. Maybe all will. Or maybe what your own Inner Patriarch says is a little different from any of these:

— An unmarried woman is an unfulfilled woman.
— A wife's job—no matter who she is or what she does—is first and foremost to take care of her husband!
— Women should never pursue men; men should always do the pursuing.
— A woman without a child has not fulfilled her destiny.
— Women should stop pretending to be men. They should stay at home and stop wanting more.
— She's a woman, and she'll never amount to anything. It's ridiculous for her to even hope for anything. Basically, she's better off not trying.
— It's too bad she was born a woman. If only she were a man, she could make use of her brains (or sports ability, or common sense, or natural aggressiveness, etc.).
— The best thing for a woman to do is find a rich husband and settle down. Women aren't good for anything else.
— Women are bitchy and "naggy" underneath. I don't like them.
— Women's hormonal imbalances make them unfit for any serious work.

— Frankly, I think a woman's job is to get a rich husband so that she can take care of her parents when they get older.
— Women are illogical.
— Women are too emotional and always overreacting.
— Women lack focus.
— Women have no sense of values. They're frivolous.
— I can't stand women's talk. It has no substance.
— Women are basically weaker than men.
— Women are irresponsible. When it comes to really important things, they cannot be trusted.
— You can never really understand a woman.
— Women are needy.
— Women have poor judgment. I'd never use a woman doctor or lawyer.
— Basically, there's only one thing they're good for and that's sex.
— Once a woman is no longer attractive and good for sex, she is basically useless.
— She doesn't have to do anything important. She's only a woman! Whatever she does is extra.
— A woman should have babies. That's what she's good for!

The statements above are isolated comments taken out of context. Now I would like you to listen to the Inner Patriarch speak. In this way, you can hear his concerns and values in his own words, rather than having me translate them for you. The following conversations, as well as conversations or comments that I will quote later in this book, have been accessed directly using Voice Dialogue.

## CARLA'S INNER PATRIARCH

Carla, an attractive, delightful, well-educated psychotherapist born in the late 1930s, attended one of our training workshops.

The following conversation with her Inner Patriarch was conducted by Mona, a member of our training staff. Carla began the session by saying that she had a headache on the left side of her head, with stiffness and pain going down into the left side of her neck and shoulder. She was feeling some kind of inner struggle building up. Carla had a sense that there was some part of herself that didn't like her being at the workshop and did not like the way she was behaving. Earlier in the day, she had gone for a walk in the beautiful countryside, but did not really feel comfortable or satisfied. She had even noticed some mental flashes where she suddenly imagined/pictured a man coming out from behind the trees and physically attacking her.

Other people had been talking about the Inner Patriarch, and Carla wondered if that had something to do with her current state of mind. Mona suggested that she facilitate Carla's Inner Patriarch. The following is the transcript of that facilitation.

> *Carla:* I'm not really sure what an Inner Patriarch is or if I have one.
>
> *Facilitator:* Let's just say it's a part of you that has very strong opinions about how you should and shouldn't behave as woman.
>
> *Carla:* Oh, I'm sure there's a part like that.
>
> *Facilitator:* Perhaps you might want to move back behind to the left in the direction of that headache.
>
> Carla moved her chair. When she sat down, it was no longer Carla, but her Inner Patriarch who spoke. He sat very straight, even rigid. He was tall and stern, and spoke with a lot of forcefulness and contained anger.
>
> *Inner Patriarch:* I have lots of rules, and first of all she should *never* go without a bra!

*Facilitator*: I see. Does she have one on today?

*Inner Patriarch*: No, she doesn't, and I don't like that at all. She could get into trouble. I don't want her to dress in any way that is sexual. She can wear some colors, but the clothes should all be very professional, nothing suggestive.

*Facilitator*: What kind of trouble could she get into?

*Inner Patriarch*: She'd get into a situation she couldn't handle; someone could attack her.

*Facilitator*: You mean physically?

*Inner Patriarch*: Yes, physically attack her.

*Facilitator*: Did you have anything to do with those flashes in her mind today when she was out walking? Do you make her think things like that to threaten her?

*Inner Patriarch*: Well, she deserves that! She has no business walking around alone. In fact, I don't really ever want her to be alone.

*Facilitator*: What are some of your other rules?

*Inner Patriarch*: Well, anything out of the 19th century. I want everything to be very traditional. I like her husband. He makes a small show of vacuuming or doing some dishes, but really he's like me. He wants her to take care of him and take care of the house. A woman should always stay a little behind the man and take care of him, take care of his physical needs and his emotions. She should do whatever it takes to keep him in good humor.

*Facilitator*: And if she doesn't do that, what happens?

*Inner Patriarch*: Well, if she doesn't do that, she might lose him. This is her third marriage, and she's 56 years old. She needs the financial security. Her husband has a retirement fund, and if she doesn't please him, she could lose him and end up alone. She could end up on the street!

*Facilitator:* You're certainly worried about some pretty serious things.

*Inner Patriarch:* Yes, and I don't like what she's doing here at all. I don't want her to get into a lot of feelings. I want all of that to be very under control.

*Facilitator:* You mentioned earlier that she should take care of the man's emotions, but I guess from what you're saying that you don't want her to express any of those feelings outwardly. It sounds like she should be a sort of shock absorber for the emotions.

*Inner Patriarch:* That's exactly right! I don't want her to be emotional and needy. She should take care of all that on the inside where it doesn't show.

*Facilitator:* I'd be interested to know where you learned all your rules for her.

*Inner Patriarch:* Well, her mother was from Mississippi and brought the whole tradition of southern white womanhood, and her father was a very traditional WASP man [said very proudly, as if he were saying he had two Ph.D.'s]. I have *two* traditions to support me!

*Facilitator:* What did you learn from her father?

*Inner Patriarch:* Well, her father is the one who said there are only three kinds of jobs that women can have. They can teach, they can help people, or be nurses.

*Facilitator*: So it's okay for her to be a therapist helping people?

*Inner Patriarch*: It's okay so long as she isn't in any position of authority or responsibility.

*Facilitator*: You mean like being a director or a leader?

*Inner Patriarch*: Yes, I don't want her to try to do anything really significant. Women can't do that. I wouldn't want her to be famous; women shouldn't be like that. And even if women do get famous, they should give it up to be with a man. Look at Jane Fonda. She had her little career, but she settled right down with an older man and gave it all up. That's the way it should be. I don't want Carla to ever be independent or famous—I wouldn't be able to stand her. I couldn't live with her. If she got too rich and famous, there'd be no place for me; I'd be gone.

This discussion provides a general sense of the power and judgments of the Inner Patriarch. We, as women, find that his disparaging comments and his feeling that women are basically inferior to men give us an uneasy feeling about ourselves and undermine our authority. Our Inner Patriarchs agree with the outer patriarchy that our contributions are unimportant and that nobody should listen to us. Carla's Inner Patriarch is a classic. You can hear his concerns, his judgments, and his fear of what will happen if he loses control of her behavior. You can also hear that he has gathered his ideas from both her father and mother. Our Inner Patriarchs are also influenced by the church and the media, by our schools and our friends, and last, but certainly not least, by the adults whose behavior we admire and want to emulate.

### An "Arab" Inner Patriarch

Although Dominique was not Arab, she had both a classical Inner Patriarch, like Carla's, and what she called an "Arab" one. Her Arab Inner Patriarch was quite lyrical about her and about everything feminine, but he kept her from going out in the world on her own and earning a living. He kept her from becoming independent. Dominique was a brilliant, articulate woman and a natural teacher, but she could only use her talents in the service of a man. I have included this particular Inner Patriarch because of his eloquence and his powerfully seductive appreciation of the feminine.

> *Sidra:* I would like to know what you think about Dominique's plans to lead workshops and earn money to support herself in a comfortable fashion.
>
> *Inner Patriarch* (lyrically and gently): I think that it is a mistake for her to go out in the world and teach. I fear that she will lose something very precious if she does that. A woman needs to be protected. She belongs inside of a house, within walls.
>
> You know, a woman is like a flower. Her essence is beautiful and powerful, but it is fragile, very fragile. If this essence is enclosed, it will bloom. If it is out in the world, it will not be able to bloom; its blossoms will be crushed.
>
> Think of it this way—a woman is like a precious jewel. If she is out in the world, she will rub up against others, and she will no longer be pristine; she will be scratched.
>
> If a woman is out in the world, her essential nature, which is like a goddess, will be sullied. She will lose her natural beauty and purity. She will lose the power of her

essential goddess energies. In a male world, she will lose her softness, and she might even become like a man.

*Sidra:* How do you feel about me? I'm out in the world.

*Inner Patriarch* (looking at me sadly and a bit wistfully): It's a shame that you have had to be out in the world so much. You are exposed to great unhappiness and suffering when you work with people. You have rubbed up against too many people and have had contact with too much pain. That is not good for a woman. I don't know how much more brilliant or powerful or beautiful you would be now if you had remained protected.

I must admit that by the time I was through talking with this particular Inner Patriarch, I was pretty well seduced! I was just about ready to end my career and allow my husband to care for me for the remainder of my life. Staying inside, avoiding all the difficulties of life in the world, and being protected because I was so precious was sounding quite attractive. But I could see that this Inner Patriarch was paralyzing Dominique. Because of his beliefs, she feared that she would lose too much and would no longer be a feminine woman if she were to go out into the world and be successful.

## Women Who Feel Superior to Other Women: A Legacy of the Inner Patriarch

Carla's Inner Patriarch does not value her above other women; he devalues all women equally. Dominique's Inner Patriarch puts her on a pedestal, but he does this for all women. Adrianne's Inner Patriarch is different. He is typical of the Inner Patriarchs found in women who have been raised in strongly patriarchal households. These women reject the weaknesses of their mothers and are highly critical of other women, particularly those who have retained their basic femininity. They see these women as weak and unimportant and ignore them. They look to men, rather than women, as teachers. They value the approval of men and ignore the approval of women, seeing this as trivial.

This reaction on the part of another woman can be confusing, and it is happening more frequently than you would ever imagine! As a woman, I might expect my opinions to be overlooked by men, but I would expect that a "sister" would listen. This is not necessarily the case.

*The Inner Patriarch operating through a woman is even more judgmental than the outer patriarch. At least the outer patriarch is in a man's body, and he responds to a woman in fairly predictable ways. As women, we are familiar with this. We know what to expect and how to deal with it. When confronted with what is essentially a judgmental man in a woman's body, matters become pretty complicated. We have a sense of discomfort, the feeling that there is probably something wrong with us as individuals and that nothing we can do will earn us this person's respect.*

I have had many uncomfortable experiences with this disapproval, and it was the exploration of these experiences that initially led me to the discovery of the workings of the Inner Patriarch in women. I am grateful to the many women who have allowed their Inner Patriarchs to be interviewed by me over the years. Many times these interviews would build upon this uncomfortable feeling that a disapproving man was looking at me through female eyes.

One of the most powerful of these Voice Dialogue sessions was with Adrienne's Inner Patriarch. Adrianne and I had known one another for a number of years. Although I respected her and admired the work she did, there was always something about Adrianne that made me uncomfortable. One day we spoke about this. Adrianne told me that she felt unsafe with me. I admitted that I had, indeed, withdrawn from her and avoided emotional intimacy.

As I thought about it, I realized that I had withdrawn from her because I sensed the presence of an extremely powerful and judgmental Inner Patriarch. As a result, I did not trust Adrianne. Together we decided that it would be a good idea to have me talk with her Inner Patriarch. We spent approximately an hour in a deep and honest exchange.

Since I was able to honor this Inner Patriarch and listen to his comments calmly and objectively, he was happy to tell me about himself. He was cool and alert and looked at me critically throughout our Voice Dialogue session. He was astute, seeming to evaluate both my reasoning and my emotional reactions. The following excerpt of our Voice Dialogue session gives a good picture of his overall reaction to me.

*Sidra:* It seems that you don't have much respect for women. Is that true?

*Inner Patriarch:* That's quite true. I don't have any respect for women. As far as I'm concerned, there is nothing that any women can teach me. I've watched them all, and none of them is worth anything, particularly the frilly, feminine ones [looks at me challengingly].

*Sidra:* (Motioning to the dress I'm wearing) Do you see me as one of the frilly ones?

*Inner Patriarch:* Yes, I do. You fix yourself up and try to look good. You wear makeup and dresses. You look feminine and for me that looks weak. It's obvious to me that Hal has all the power and the knowledge and that you just lean on him. I don't want to be bothered with you. I want to go to the source. I only put up with you because I have to in order to work with Hal. He's a man, and I respect him!

*Sidra:* Would it be better if I were less feminine? Would you respect me more if I didn't wear makeup or skirts?

*Inner Patriarch:* No, that wouldn't help at all. You would just be another one of those women pretending that you're as good as a man. That doesn't work, you know. You're not a man. I do have to admit that your teaching has improved over the years. You've actually become quite good. Impersonal and objective.

*Sidra:* Do you watch me and evaluate me when I'm teaching?

*Inner Patriarch:* Of course I do. I'm always there. I watch everything you say and what you do. I am always waiting for you to slip. I can see those times when you are "on" and those times when you are more unsure of yourself. I watch for inconsistencies, and when I find them, I really judge you. I just wait for you to do something wrong, to say something inconsistent, or to do a less perfect presentation than you did yesterday. I truly enjoy each shortcoming that I find [said in a self-satisfied, triumphant voice].

*Sidra:* So I have to do everything perfectly each time?

*Inner Patriarch:* Yes, you do. You must do everything absolutely perfectly.

*Sidra:* What about Hal? Do you watch him as well?

*Inner Patriarch:* Yes, I do.

*Sidra:* Do you notice inconsistencies there? Do you judge him when he is less than perfect?

*Inner Patriarch:* I notice that sometimes he does a great job and sometimes he's a bit off. I can see his inconsistencies and that from time to time he leaves out something important. But that doesn't matter at all. Those are just the natural variations from one teaching session to the next. He knows what he's doing even if it isn't perfect.

*Sidra:* So you have different standards for us?

*Inner Patriarch:* Of course I do. He's a man, he has a lot to say, and he should be saying it. You're a woman, and a woman shouldn't be teaching. You should be at home with your children, not in front of a group. As I said before, I'm just not interested in listening to a woman.

Looking at the above exchange, the basic issue is not the question of fairness or equality. The issue here is one of awareness. We, as women, must become aware of the operation of this Inner Patriarch. It is extremely important to bring his reactions out into the light of day so that they can be dealt with openly. When Adrianne's Inner Patriarch was operating unconsciously, he was continually pummeling me, and neither Adrianne nor I knew this. All we knew was that something was creating an uncomfortable distance between us and we were not able to work together with mutual respect and trust. This is not at all uncommon. Many women who do not wish to work with other women, but prefer to work with men, have very powerful Inner Patriarchs similar to Adrianne's.

Once the role of the Inner Patriarch became apparent, Adrianne and I were able to establish a far more intimate connection that felt very pleasant to both of us. We were free to be with one another in a natural way and to react to one another, both positively and negatively, with objectivity. We were able, for the first time, to really enjoy one another!

## Men Have Inner Patriarchs, Too

I will be concentrating upon the Inner Patriarchs of the women in our culture because they operate in the shadows. We do not know about them; we do not hear what they say. They exist outside of our awareness, but nonetheless we respond to them. We listen to their injunctions and opinions, but we do not know that this is what we are doing. What we do know is that we sometimes feel bad about ourselves without any apparent reason; we tend to stop our natural way of being in this world, and we may respond to men as though they had dominion over us. We do not feel entitled. We also know that when both a woman and a man are present, we tend to pay more attention and give more weight to whatever it is that the man has to say.

The patriarchal voice of the man in our culture is more apparent to everyone. He does not operate in the shadows; he operates quite openly. In fact, his views, at least until recently, have been the foundation of the attitudes, values, and laws of our society.

*The Patriarch in men is proud to be a man, and he claims the rights that are associated with this pride. These rights include a natural authority and privilege. The Patriarch of the man expects to be listened to. He knows what he knows, and he expects others to pay attention to him. He expects women to defer to him and to serve him, but if he meets a woman who is objective and sure of herself, a woman who has many of the same qualities that he admires in himself and in other men, he may respect her in the same way that he respects other men. However, not all Patriarchs are alike in men or in women, and there are some who will never respect a woman, any woman at all, just because she is a woman.*

The Patriarch in the man also carries a set of rules regarding his responsibilities to women. *He is the archetypal father. He dominates and he demands respect, but he protects those in his care and is responsible for their safety and well-being.* He will do whatever it is that he has to do, even though this may stretch him beyond his natural boundaries. I have often heard these patriarchs in men sound exhausted, totally worn out by the demands made upon them by their own rules and requirements.

I would like to give you a chance to hear two contrasting Patriarchs in two very different men. The first is more fearsome and judgmental; the second is more supportive and objective. They represent two extremes in the way that the Patriarch in a man relates to women and to the man's responsibilities towards them.

## Stuart's Patriarch

Stuart is a traditional man raised in a very traditional religious background. He is divorced from his first wife, and he supports her and the children that they had together. He sees himself as a person with unquestioned authority—the person who is ultimately responsible for everything and everyone. Stuart is not happy about feeling this way, but his Patriarch is a primary self (one who dominates his thinking and his behavior in life), and this Patriarch says that a man's responsibility is his responsibility. Stuart is extremely judgmental about anyone who is not as strong and responsible as he is, and he is particularly angry about women whom he sees as exploitative and useless.

Stuart's Patriarch does not equivocate on the topic of women. He says, "I don't like women. Not at all. They are sneaky and useless, and they are always manipulating Stuart to get what they want. He's a fool around them. They all start out sweet and sexy, and they seduce him. They pretend that they are nice and strong and independent, but do you know what they want?" He continues angrily without waiting for an answer. "What they really want is to take him for all he's got. They know that he's a sucker. They want his money. They want him to support them. None of them wants to work. They're all lazy."

This Patriarch has some very high standards for Stuart. He explains how Stuart must be strong and uncomplaining: "If a man does not meet his responsibilities, I have no respect for him. I don't care whether or not he is sick. I don't want to hear if he is capable of what he is asked to do. He just has to do what he has to do. If the man falls apart, everything around him will fall apart. You know, his grandfather was a man I admired. I heard a lot about him when we were growing up. He was a pioneer, and he brought his family out West. He worked very, very hard and suffered great hardships, but because of his bravery and his strength, the family survived. If he had been a wimp, they would have all died! I hold him up to Stuart as an example of a real man. I don't think that Stuart is as strong as he was. That grandfather of his dominated everyone and everything!"

In contrast, Hank's Patriarch feels that his job is protecting women and helping them to achieve the most that they can. He, too, sees women as basically weaker than men, and he worries about their emotionality, their weakness, and their lack of objectivity. But when he meets a woman who can be objective and empowered while still retaining her basic femininity, he respects her as he would respect a man. Unlike Stuart's Patriarch, he does not expect all women to be ineffectual.

Hank's Patriarch speaks with the same ring of authority and power as Stuart's. Both demand attention and respect from their listeners. As Hank's Patriarch puts it, "I know what I know, and I'm happy to tell you about it. Just ask me anything. But I warn you, I don't like to be manipulated, and I expect you to listen to me. Actually, to tell the truth, I am not very interested in what you have to say if you don't agree with me." He goes on to explain that the reason that people don't listen to women is that women don't have his voice speaking out for them. If women used their Inner Patriarchs for the authority they carry, rather than fight them, people would listen to them.

Unlike Stuart's Patriarch, Hank's differentiates among women. He does not think that they are all doomed to uselessness, and he sees their potential strengths. He feels responsible for keeping them safe and helping them grow. However, unlike Stuart's, he is not committed to the idea that Hank would always be financially and emotionally responsible for the women in his life. When asked about his views on women and power, he says: "I admire a woman who can stand up to me and talk to me, a woman who is like me and knows what she knows. I have no respect for women who become victims or who are defensive and attacking. If a woman has her power, that's fine with me. I can't hand them that power; they have to get it for themselves, but I will respect it when it is there. I feel safer with a woman who is objective and powerful. She doesn't need to prove anything with me, so she does not need to attack me."

Hank's Patriarch is particularly eloquent when he speaks about morality and sexuality. He has definite views on protecting the virtue of women and the sanctity of marriage. "I keep him monogamous, you know. Without me inside of him telling him what to do, Hank, and other men like him, would be sexually involved with every woman he meets. I'm the one with the rules against incest. Without me, men, and women too, would be out of control. Women should be happy that I'm around. I make life safe for them, and I protect the family. I think that's very important. I resent it when women speak negatively of me. I think that I do a lot for them."

As Hank's Patriarch speaks, it is apparent that he admires and supports the women around him when he feels they are doing their share of the work. He sees it as his mission to use his superior strength and his natural power to protect their natural areas of vulnerability and to help them succeed in the world. However, he wants them to remain women. He has no respect for a woman who has too many masculine characteristics. In contrast to Stuart's Patriarch, Hanks is happy to grant women respect, independence, and power if they prove themselves worthy.

I have given these two examples of Patriarchs in men to show you the range of beliefs and behaviors that you might encounter. No book on the Inner Patriarch can overlook the fact that he is alive in men as well as in women. However, from now on, I will be talking about the Inner Patriarchs I have met in women. Before we go any further, I would like to introduce you to a very special kind of Inner Patriarch, one that I have often encountered in women who are on a spiritual path.

### The Spiritualized Inner Patriarch

Some Inner Patriarchs, both in women and men, have a primarily spiritual orientation. They see God and all his emissaries as male. There is no room for women in sacred spaces. However, there is a place for women in their world view. These Inner Patriarchs see the proper path for a truly evolved woman as different from the path of the ordinary, inferior woman. In order to obey the dictates of this particular Inner Patriarch, the superior woman turns her back on ordinary female-oriented matters. She foregoes relationship, sexuality, motherhood, power, and all the joy, pain, and turmoil that these areas contribute to life.

Instead, she avoids the pitfalls of the female fate and devotes herself to higher matters. When she does so, her Inner Patriarch is satisfied. Like Teresa of Avila, she transforms her sexuality and her passions into a love of God. She is likely to remain abstinent for long periods of time, if not forever.

*If this woman finds her own place with an appropriate guru, priest, or teacher, her Inner Patriarch is content. He supports her complete devotion to the outer patriarch, in the form of her teacher, who always seems to know what is best for her. In this way, she does not have to assume responsibility for herself and her actions, and she will not make womanly errors. Her Inner Patriarch feels that he has done his job well and that she will be safe both in this world and the next.*

### Becoming a Man to Fight the Patriarchy

*Some women disown their sexuality and their womanliness in order to deal effectively with these negative attitudes about women and every-*

*thing womanly.* Gertrude was one of these women. She was raised to be a good daughter by a father who was a strong patriarch, and she dutifully married a patriarch just like him and became "daughter" to her husband. Gertrude's Inner Patriarch tried to support her by not letting the fact that she was born a woman interfere with her life. In a very successful attempt to rescue her from being "just a housewife," he made her a better man than any of them. He insisted that she complete a rigorous Ph.D. at a German university, and as the years passed, she finally became the only tenured woman on the university staff. It was fascinating to talk with her Inner Patriarch. These are some of the comments he made about her:

— I was always upset about her being in a woman's body. I made sure that she was never stopped by being a woman. When her mother told her that she wouldn't be able to think well enough to take examinations when she was menstruating, I told her to do them anyway. I made her travel all over and do anything a man could do. I made her do it faster and better. Even her father had to respect her.

— I'm very uneasy about women. They don't seem to have any control, and they're very unpredictable. I know how things are and how they should be, and when she listens to me, she does what she should do and it comes out well.

— She's doing all this goddess work, and I'm uncomfortable about it. It feels silly to me. She shouldn't pray to a goddess. God is a man, and that's all there is to it. I feel very foolish when she does otherwise.

— I'm afraid when she doesn't have a goal to move towards. I don't know what she'll do.

I spoke with Gertrude's Inner Patriarch for quite some time. He was fascinating. Soon he realized that I did not judge him and I was not out to destroy him, and he mellowed perceptibly. He, however, was still very afraid of the emotional and creative sides of her. He said, "I'm afraid that she'll lose status if she starts to develop her creativity; she'll just be looked upon as another woman doing foolish things. All the prestige and power that I've gained for her over the years will be gone. *Nobody will respect her anymore if she doesn't behave as I tell her to, if she stops acting like a man and starts acting like a woman!*"

One of the problems here is that Gertrude is not allowed to be a woman and to develop her more feminine aspects. This cuts her off from many of her natural inclinations and joys. In addition, however much she may behave like a man, she is still a woman, and this basic fact is problematical.

I have given you a general picture of the Inner Patriarch. Let us now consider each of the areas of his concern in greater detail. In the following chapter, I will quote more Inner Patriarchs, and you will have the opportunity to hear them and to see if any of their comments sound familiar. This will enable you to tune into your own Inner Patriarch and to listen for his views on women.

*Until you hear the Inner Patriarch's comments in this context, you will have difficulty perceiving them as separate from yourself. You are like a fish who swims in the water of our dominant culture. A fish swimming in water cannot describe the water until she gets out of it.* So, read on and separate from the water in which we have all been swimming.

# IN HIS OWN WORDS:

## A Detailed Account of the Beliefs and Values of the Inner Patriarch

# THE INNER PATRIARCH AND POWER

*I feel totally hopeless, doomed. I am a woman.*
*Whatever I do, I cannot win.*
                    — from Irene's dream

Where do our Inner Patriarchs get their basic training? *It is our mothers, repeating the values of a patriarchal culture, who have taught our Inner Patriarchs much of what they know and believe.* Why would our mothers do this when it undermines our power? As they see it, they are teaching us how to get along in a "man's world." In all truth, these teachings can be quite helpful at times, but it is important for us to look at how they hold us back. As adult women, we can reclaim our power or, for some of us, we can experience it for the first time when we learn to listen for this voice within us and evaluate its input.

### The Inner Patriarch and Power

The Inner Patriarch does not want a woman to assume a position of power in the world. It may be acceptable for her to be powerful in the home, but never outside of it. *He feels that power belongs to men in the natural order of things. This objection to power in women runs very, very deep. It almost feels cellular, as though it has been programmed into our DNA.* I sometimes wonder whether this dread of women's power originates in our history. After all, what happened to most women of power in the past? The ancient priestesses were

murdered as "idolaters" and "heathen," and the wise and powerful women in more recent centuries were burned as witches. The
lesson that being powerful is not safe has been transmitted by our
culture and by our mothers

The following dream provides a picture of this power issue and
how our Inner Patriarchs are trained by our mothers. It was dreamt
during a workshop at which I taught about the Inner Patriarch.
The woman who dreamed it is Dutch and in her early forties. She
is intelligent, multilingual, psychologically sophisticated, and quite
worldly, having lived in America, Canada, Africa, and France. She
is certainly not someone who is afraid to try anything new!

## IRENE'S DREAM

*I am in my parental home with the entire family. I have just
received a booklet telling me that I have been accepted into an
important university. I go to the living room and leave the
booklet lying about on the couch. My mother is sitting on her
brother's knees on that couch, and two other brothers are
standing close to her. They are telling her that she is no good
and never will be, that she is a stupid woman. I see how hurt
she feels, how humiliated and hurt. One moment later, she
picks up my booklet, reads it, and looks at me.*

*Now my mother's face begins to look different. Her eyes
are cold and extremely distant, as if she is wearing a very stiff,
withdrawn mask. She's my mother, and yet she is not.* [Note:
It is no longer Irene's mother, but the mother's Inner Patriarch who is now speaking.] *This new mother frightens
me, she is too cold, too far away, totally out of touch with my
feelings or needs. I am smiling at her to please her, to melt her,
hoping it will work, but she gives no sign that she even notices.
She stares at me coldly, lifts up the booklet with her right hand
and asks me, "What is this nonsense?" I tell her how important it is to me, but she says, "It's absolutely worthless.*

*This is a degree from an American university. They are worth nothing."*

*I feel very bad. I wish she would, just once in her life, support or admire my decisions. I ask her if it would be better if it were a Dutch university. "That's impossible. You're too old. You can forget about studying at 42."*

*"What if I were 19?" I asked.*

*"Nineteen?" she asks. "At nineteen you should be thinking about getting yourself a husband and having children!" I feel totally hopeless, doomed. I am a woman; whatever I do, I cannot win. I realize, however, that this is not just my mother rejecting her daughter. It is a hurt person, giving the message she received, passing it on to me. Knowing it comes from that source, I feel less hurt, somehow less involved, more independent.*

*I turn my back on this woman and walk away. A woman friend stands behind me, suddenly she backs me up, her right hand and my left hand intertwine. I know her from a Voice Dialogue workshop, and I like her a lot. This shared energy and strength feels very good. I thank her.*

*I then leave the house and, as I leave it, I discover that the world outside is no longer horizontal; it is now sideways. I must learn a new way to walk in this world.*

This is a beautiful picture of how our Inner Patriarch receives his teachings from our mothers. Our mothers were hurt by the outer patriarchal attitudes of a culture that devalued the feminine. They were humiliated if they strove for power, if they moved beyond the aspirations that were permitted them. The outer patriarchy (in this dream, the brothers) shamed them for this and for being women. In order to spare us this humiliation, they taught us to limit ourselves.

Thus, it is our own limited expectations, as defined by the Inner Patriarch, which match the defined limitations of the culture. We agree that we should not aspire to too much power, that this is dangerous. Even if we are given power, now that the outer world has changed somewhat, we are uncomfortable as long as our Inner Patriarchs worry about this issue. As I have said, they feel that power is a serious issue, so let us listen to how they speak of this in their own words.

### The Inner Patriarch Speaks of a Woman's Power

The following are comments made by the Inner Patriarchs of American, Australian, and European women:

— A real woman doesn't want power!
— Women should not be in a position of power because it violates the natural order of things.
— If she takes her power, she's acting like a man and she's not really a woman.
— Women just don't do things like that. No, I'm not proud of her [said about a woman who has set up a large, extremely successful business].
— She's a woman, and she'll never amount to much. It's ridiculous for her to even hope for anything. Basically, she's better off not trying.
— She's a woman. She shouldn't even try. She'll just fall on her face.
— She must have slept with someone to get where she is.
— Yes, she did build up a big business, but she's only a woman and I'm afraid it will fall apart.
— No matter what she does, she'll always be second, so she should just relax and admit it and she'll feel better.
— Women's businesses never work out. They're okay for little boutiques, but that's all.
— It's just a fluke [about a woman's major success in a traditionally male job].

48

## The Glass Ceiling

*The glass ceiling is not just outside, but within us. The Inner Patriarch will literally trip us up when we have reached some major achievement. Its fear is that we will take too much power, that we will be too dominant and that, as a result, we will be exposed to either humiliation or actual danger.*

During one of my talks on the Inner Patriarch, a woman who was quite active nationally in the National Executives Association made the observation that at a recent national convention, she had noted a surprising number of women who had broken arms, legs, or ankles that were due to falls. She wondered, quite astutely, whether this might be the result of their Inner Patriarch's actually "tripping them up" as they reached national prominence. This seemed like a very good hypothesis.

Patsy Schiff, an attorney and mediator, spoke of the Inner Patriarch's role in undermining women's power and success, what I think of as "the inner glass ceiling." The following is an excerpt from a talk called "Conflict Within and Without," which she gave to a woman's network in Sacramento, on October 7, 1992. She described it in this way:

> *I am often reminded of what [Hal and Sidra Stone] call the Inner Patriarch...This self believes that women can't really do anything as well as men—so, for example, you might have a need to go to a male surgeon if there were a serious problem. This self might think that women can't be as powerful as men when they negotiate. That self will not feel as powerful as your counterpart if you are in conflict with a man. [This would make you weaker in negotiating than you would normally be.] As great as our strides have been as women, there still is a patriarchal view that is prevalent in society. [And, as we have seen, in the Inner Patriarchs of women.] A study of mediator success in a recent* Mediation Quarterly *showed that male*

*and female mediators had equivalent rates of success, but that female mediators had higher success rates in fashioning settlements that lasted. Interestingly, the clients' perception was that female mediators were less competent—even when they felt the results were more successful.*

Our Inner Patriarchs, as we have heard from their previous comments, totally agree with this point of view. Whatever it is that a woman does, a man either has done it better or could do it better. Inner Patriarchs talking about women doctors make such comments as:

— Do you really trust a woman doctor? I don't.
— She probably only works part-time and doesn't keep up with things
— Women can be doctors, but not really.

I have seen many examples of women who have attained their career objectives after battling the outer male-dominated world, only to be faced with their Inner Patriarchs, their own inner glass ceiling.

Connie, who had earned her Ph.D. in Economics, a male-dominated field, was awarded an excellent assignment in Cambodia, a job for which she was uniquely qualified. She was delighted and ready to take advantage of this opportunity. Her Inner Patriarch, however, was unimpressed. His comment was, "Are you sure that you can do this? You're just a girl!"

Ruth, who had fought her way through architectural school, gotten a job during the recession, learned how to behave appropriately in an office of patriarchal males, and had finally been awarded a major contract to design a medical school lab in Zimbabwe, was excited. All her hard work had paid off. Her Inner Patriarch's comment was, "Are you sure that they shouldn't be putting a man on this job? It might be too much for you."

## The Inner Patriarch Speaks Out on Power and Relationship

Alma is an attractive 31-year-old woman who has enjoyed amazing success as an entrepreneur. She thinks of herself as a feminist and was greatly encouraged by both of her parents to follow this course in her life. She has no conscious awareness of an Inner Patriarch. She has devoted her energies to her work at the expense of a personal life up until now. As Alma moves toward relationships, we interview her Inner Patriarch to find out what he has to say about the "Rules of Relationships and Power."

*Sidra:* It seems to me that you have some rules about relationships.

*Inner Patriarch:* You bet I do. When she gets into a relationship, I expect her to walk to the right of the man and about one step behind him. She should never walk at his side or look as though she wants to be his equal. Men don't like that, and I don't approve.

*Sidra:* How do you feel about her success in the world?

*Inner Patriarch:* As far as I'm concerned, she is a failure. She is obviously a flawed woman because she has never been able to have or maintain a relationship with a man. None of what she has done in her life impresses me at all.

*Sidra:* How would you feel if she were a man, had reached the age of 31, and was successful in business, but had not yet made a good and lasting relationship?

*Inner Patriarch:* That would be a different story. If she were a man, she'd have plenty of time. As it is, she'd better hurry.

*Sidra:* So, you are in hurry?

51

*Inner Patriarch:* Yes, I am.

*Sidra:* Does that have anything to do with wanting this current relationship to grow and evolve?

*Inner Patriarch:* Yes, she'd better get something to work soon.

*Sidra:* Oh, have you been involved in others? Like the last one where she had some question about how appropriate he was?

*Inner Patriarch:* Yes. I am the one who tells her not to worry; it will be all right. I feel that if she tries hard enough, it will work out. I do get very nervous when I think of her not being in a relationship.

*Sidra:* Again, would this worry you if she were a man?

*Inner Patriarch:* No.

*Sidra:* But she can earn a really good living. She can take care of herself.

*Inner Patriarch:* That's not enough; a woman should be a wife, and that's all there is to it.

*Sidra:* How do you feel about her being a mother?

*Inner Patriarch:* I don't care as much about that. Just a wife.

*Sidra:* We've been talking about her neediness. How do you feel about that?

*Inner Patriarch:* She can be a little bit needy, but not enough to drain him. He needs all his energy to get things done in the world.

*Sidra:* So, you would expect her to support him?

*Inner Patriarch:* Yes. I'd expect her to put him first, to make a good, comfortable home for him, good meals—a nest that will keep him safe and refreshed so that he'd be able to go out again the next day and work.

*Sidra:* Then, her work would be unimportant?

*Inner Patriarch:* Yes. His is what's important.

*Sidra:* What about her feelings? It's taken her a long time to learn about them.

*Inner Patriarch:* She can share a little with him to make the relationship good, but I wouldn't want her burdening him with her feelings. She should talk to her girlfriends about them. Especially if she's unhappy. That's what girlfriends are for. She has a few good friends; she should keep her feelings with them. Men shouldn't be burdened with a woman's feelings. They have important work to do.

*Sidra:* Again, her work doesn't really matter to you?

*Inner Patriarch:* I told you already; her work doesn't matter. What matters to me is that she has a relationship!

No matter what Alma does in her professional life, her Inner Patriarch remains unimpressed. He will not be happy until she is properly married. Nothing less will do. However, if Alma were to abandon her successful professional life and become a full-time wife and, perhaps, a mother, her Inner Patriarch would lose all respect for her and become disdainful. Here again is the "Catch-22" of the Inner Patriarch!

*As you have seen, the Inner Patriarch sees power in women as an unnatural occurrence that makes a woman unfeminine and interferes with her ability to relate to men. For him, the expression "a feminine woman of power" is an oxymoron.* In addition to his other concerns, he is afraid that if women take full power, they will no longer be females and will no longer need or want men. This is not necessarily true, and I will be talking more about how to retain femininity while taking power in a later chapter. First, however, let us look at the Inner Patriarch's feelings and rules about relationships, particularly traditional ones between men and women.

# THE INNER PATRIARCH AND RELATIONSHIP

*I don't care what she has accomplished in her
lifetime. A woman without a husband is a failure!*
— an Inner Patriarch

Relationship is extremely important to the Inner Patriarch! The continuity and the success of male/female relationships is his major concern. *His job is to promote and protect heterosexual relationships and marriage and, through these, the continuity of the culture.* I have had the opportunity to talk with the Inner Patriarchs of a number of lesbian women, and almost all of them were very judgmental about homosexuality. At the same time that these women were coping with the often homophobic reactions of a patriarchal culture, they were dealing with their own Inner Patriarch's painful attacks from within. Until they learned about, and separated from, their Inner Patriarchs, they thought that all the negative judgments came from the outside. After hearing their Inner Patriarchs, they were aware that they needed to protect themselves on two fronts rather than one.

*Even an Inner Patriarch who has changed his views on all other aspects of a woman's behavior usually has something to say about a woman's role in relationship.* His expectations, injunctions, rules, and judgments have most often been transmitted by the mother—not the father—to both her daughters and her sons. The mother does not always transmit these ideas verbally; often she models them,

55

sometimes commenting upon her own behavior or other women's, and using these behaviors as an example to follow or avoid.

The Inner Patriarch has definitive views about relationship and a woman's role within relationship. *He considers relationship a woman's area of expertise–something that is basically her responsibility. He exalts her role in relationship and gives credit to her for maintaining the quality of relationship with her husband.* Actually, he can become quite lyrical when he talks about this. In a later chapter, we will emphasize the positive aspects of this admiration and concern. In this chapter, I will concentrate upon his rules, the general devaluation of relationship-tending as an important aspect of life, and the double standard of behavior for men and women.

It is apparent from talking to the Inner Patriarch, or for that matter from observing the dominant culture, that although relationships are very, very important, they are not so important in terms of overall worldly achievement. The time spent by women tending to their relationships and the resultant quality of these relationships produces accomplishments that are basically intangible. This is definitely less valuable than "making it in the world."

When you stop to think about it, a woman who has followed the Inner Patriarch's rules and nurtured a great relationship is not admired for having accomplished something special as a result of having worked very hard. It is quite likely that she will not even be given credit for her remarkable achievement. She is seen merely as having fulfilled herself as a woman.

It is interesting to note that a man who spends a lot of time and effort nurturing a relationship is not necessarily given credit for this either. In fact, he might be viewed by some as less than manly because he is concentrating his efforts in areas that are womanly and, therefore, less important than more masculine concerns. Last but not least, it is hard to imagine anyone thinking that a man who has succeeded in creating a great relationship has fulfilled himself as a man.

I have talked to many Inner Patriarchs and would like to repeat some of the comments that they've made on relationship. *The basic premise is that any woman who is really a woman will have a husband or at least a serious boyfriend.* This first set of comments is about the absolute necessity of having a relationship with a man:

— I've told her many times: a woman without a man is not really a woman.

— She really doesn't have to do anything in life but get married and stay married—otherwise she's a failure.

— I want the strongest, most powerful, richest man for her, someone who can protect her in the world and who will be respected by other men.

— She should settle for the best available deal rather than to remain independent.

— She must be married to a man. It's a disgrace that she is a lesbian!

— A woman needs a strong male to protect her.

*Once the woman is in a relationship, the Inner Patriarch makes sure that she takes full responsibility for both the relationship and the man.* It works something like this: Jane and Joe, who are husband and wife, meet back at home after a day of work. Joe is withdrawn and cold, apparently disturbed about something. Jane's Inner Patriarch immediately begins to review the events of the morning and the previous night to see what she might have done wrong that made him unhappy. Obviously, she is responsible for his bad mood. Her Inner Patriarch questions her: "Did you say anything?" "Were you loving enough at breakfast?" He makes observations such as: "You know, you were too tired to make love last night. He's probably angry with you." By the time her Inner Patriarch is through cross-examining her, Jane is likely to feel so guilty that she will not be able to relate naturally and comfortably to Joe. She will not be able to partner him.

If the situation is reversed, if Jane comes home withdrawn and apparently disturbed, the scenario is likely to be different. Joe, not having an Inner Patriarch that makes him responsible for Jane, assumes that something has happened at work and is free to ask her about it. Since his Inner Patriarch does not hold him responsible for Jane's moods, he can be more objective about the situation and not feel responsible for it. Interestingly enough, without these rules of responsibility, he is actually in a position to be more of a partner.

Now let's look at some of the ways in which the Inner Patriarch makes the woman responsible for her man and for the relationship. The following comments reveal his views on this very important topic:

— I think that anything wrong in a relationship is the fault of the woman. It's always her problem. I ask her questions such as: "What are you not doing for your husband that makes him unhappy (or makes him beat you)? What could you do to make things better?"

— If your man is not sexually aroused, you must have done something wrong. It's your job to restore his sexuality.

— A man needs sexual fulfillment. If a wife does not desire her husband sexually, I think that he is entitled to become involved with someone else.

— If the relationship goes sour, or moves toward divorce, I try to figure out what she did wrong or what she might do to improve matters.

— When I'm with a group of people, I look at the men. If they look happy and healthy, I think that they have good wives. If they don't look good, I know it's the woman's fault. She's just not doing her job. I blame the wife if any man is unhealthy or unhappy!

— The quality of life really depends upon the woman.

*The Inner Patriarch is an expert on how to take care of a man once you have him!* Here are some of the rules that I have heard both here in America and abroad:

— The woman is here to take care of the man.
— A woman must not outshine her man or he will leave her.
— Ideas are better if they come from your husband. Even if they are yours, make it look like he thought of them first.
— No matter what either of you do in the world, you are responsible for the home, for food, for cleanliness, and for ambiance. This is even true if you are working and he is staying home.
— A good wife is always sexually available and responsive, but never sexually demanding.
— You must always return home before the man, no matter how important your own work. It's best if it looks as though you have never been away.
— A good wife keeps her home and finances tidy.
— The most important thing is to make your husband look good! You can do this by looking good yourself, by raising obedient children, or by using his money to make your home look fine.
— Always look up to your husband, and value his opinion above yours. Know that he is smarter than you are and has more experience than you do.
— A real woman knows how to be there to support others.
— The woman must defer to her husband's needs.
— A good woman never plans any activities that will make her man uncomfortable.
— Always be sure he is asleep before you fall asleep.
— A good wife is seductive only at home with her husband, never in public.
— A wife should be at home when her husband is.

### The Inner Patriarch Describes His Ideal Marriage

The following dialogue was with the Inner Patriarch of a young, bright, attractive married woman. Annie was a graduate student in psychology.

*Sidra:* Tell me your ideas about how their [Annie and her husband's] marriage should work.

*Inner Patriarch:* I want her to be feminine. I want her to be in the background and her husband in the foreground [motions to show positions]. I like it when he's between her and the world. I don't want her facing the world alone, and I certainly don't want her to be in front of him. It's safer and more comfortable this way. No, it's right this way. That's the way it should be, and I want her to behave appropriately.

*Sidra:* What do you mean by "appropriately"?

*Inner Patriarch:* I know that she's smarter than her husband, and I must say that I look down on him for that, but despite this, she must appear less important than he is.

*Sidra:* How do you do that?

*Inner Patriarch:* For instance, I don't like the fact that she has to control and direct the finances, but I make sure that it looks as though he's making all the decisions. That way, if anything goes wrong, like if a check bounces, I can blame it on him. It was his decision.

Basically, I like him to make all the decisions. She cares too much about what people think. This way, if anyone doesn't like what she does, it's all her husband's fault and he has to face the music. She gets away scot-free. If she were stronger and if what people thought didn't matter as much, I'd allow her to make decisions.

*Sidra:* Where did you learn all this?

*Inner Patriarch:* I learned from her sister. Her mother was a more masculine type of person, very judgmental and unfeminine. Her sister was a model and knew how to act like a woman. So I said to her, "Take a lesson from your sister and learn how to be a woman. I know what works, and I know what men like, so listen to me and I'll make things safe for you. I really know how things work in this world. Her mother didn't know, and those feminists don't know."

*Sidra:* So you don't like feminists?

*Inner Patriarch:* I must say that in a way I admire the feminists, and I think that they're doing a good job with violence against women and rape. But they don't know how a real woman should act, and I think that they make a lot of trouble for a lot of women.

Annie was a very feminine woman who blossomed in her role as wife. She enjoyed the protection of her husband, even though she realized that much of what she was feeling was more illusory than real. But Annie's husband was not as well educated as she was, and he could be manipulated easily. He was a lesser man than her Inner Patriarch and, as a result, her Inner Patriarch had lost respect for him.

### Men Should Act Like Men

The Inner Patriarch, as you might already have guessed, is not particularly interested in the equality of the sexes. He has definite opinions about the way women should act in relationship, as you have heard, and he also has very definite feelings about the way men should be—that is, traditional males who adhere to the established masculine role. They should be powerful, assertive, dominant, rational, and ultimately responsible. Men should act like men and not like wimps.

Relationships have become fairly confusing for both men and women as their gender roles are less well defined. These days, most women would like men to have some degree of sensitivity and to be in touch with their own feelings. They like a man to know how he feels and to express this. It's wonderful to be able to communicate at the deeper feeling and spiritual levels; it is marvelous if a man is so in touch with his pain that he can cry. This is all very well and good, but the Inner Patriarchs of these same women want their men to be men. They have no respect for a man who feels intensely, and they cannot tolerate a man's tears!

*Thus, when a woman gets exactly what she wants in terms of a sensitive man who's in touch with his feelings, her Inner Patriarch is horrified. When the man feels pain, is helpless, or cries, the woman finds herself cringing. This is a shock to the woman, and it feels like a betrayal to the man who, with her encouragement, has worked so hard to get in touch with his feelings. At this particular time in history, the Inner Patriarch is the source of many of the double messages in relationships involving men and women. It's not a double message, though—not really. It is just that there are two different selves operating simultaneously. One is the encouraging, accepting, loving woman, and the other is the Inner Patriarch. Each has a very clear single message. The two just happen to conflict!*

### The Inner Patriarch's Role in Relationship

It is apparent that the Inner Patriarch does much to promote relationship. He tries his best to give advice that will work. He is very judgmental if relationships fail. *Most Inner Patriarchs are unforgiving about divorce. I have spoken with the Inner Patriarchs of women as*

*long as 25 years after a divorce and they were still angry at the woman.*
They say: "I will never forgive her for allowing her marriage to
fail!" The Inner Patriarch is likely to feel this way even if the relationship was abusive or if the divorce worked out well by any objective standards. I have heard this even where the original
marriage was brief and there were no children involved; where
both partners have married again, and have been living for long
periods in successful new marriages with happy children.

An important component of any primary relationship is sexuality. However, the Inner Patriarch's views on sexuality are so influential in our lives and relationships that I have not included
them in this discussion. Instead, I have devoted the next chapter
to them.

# THE INNER PATRIARCH AND SEXUALITY

*I dreamt that I was dancing a wonderful Dionysian dance in a beautiful palace like Versailles. I was happy and free. Then the nurses, following the orders of some man higher up, came and put me into a wheelchair and I had to stay there. I could not dance anymore.*
— from Claire's dream

This is the dream of Claire, a very successful woman lawyer, but it could be the dream of any woman with a strong Inner Patriarch. Here again we have the picture of women transmitting the Inner Patriarch's message. It is the nurses, not the male doctors, who are putting Claire into the wheelchair and stifling her female exuberance and, of course, her sexuality.

When I asked Claire's Inner Patriarch about this matter, he said that he did not want her to be sexual, that maintaining control of her sexuality and being a lawyer was her destiny. He did not want her to be distracted from her path; he wanted her to follow her destiny. In actuality, Claire's Inner Patriarch had been terrified of her sexuality ever since she'd been a little girl, and he had always done everything that he could to dampen it.

## How Does the Inner Patriarch Feel About Women's Sexuality?

Claire's Inner Patriarch had his own specific reason for controlling sexuality. He spoke about her destiny. But beneath that is his discomfort. He is not alone. *Almost every Inner Patriarch that I have heard is extremely uncomfortable with female sexuality. Basically, they do not want women to be sexual; unless, of course, it is in the service of men. The Inner Patriarchs find women's sexuality offensive and disgusting and, when they are questioned in more detail, they usually say that they find it terrifying. They often feel that men are helpless victims of a woman's sexuality.*

If a woman is sexual, then the man must automatically respond; he cannot help himself, except if he is a saint, and those are pretty rare these days. This male helplessness in the face of a woman's charms is a timeless theme. We see it beautifully illustrated in the Greek classic, the *Odyssey*. There are two episodes in which the sexual attractions of women are dangerous. The first is the story of Circe, the beautiful enchantress who enticed Ulysses' men and then, when they ate at her table, she turned them all into pigs. The second is the story of the Sirens, who sang irresistible songs and lured sailors on the passing ships. When the sailors changed course to move towards these songs, their ships crashed upon hidden rocks, and all those on board lost their lives. A woman's sexuality, her Siren song, is indeed a powerful and dangerous thing!

*However, this danger is not usually what we hear from the Inner Patriarch. Most of the Inner Patriarchs I have met concentrate upon making negative comments about women's sexuality. They are outspoken in their views of the degrading (and service) aspects of female sexuality,* making statements such as:

— Women's sexuality is disgusting!
— Her sexuality makes her look cheap.
— There's no point to her sexuality unless it turns on a man.

— If she turns on a man, she has to follow through and satis-fy him.
— She must be sexually aroused because it pleases her man.
— If she' pretty and she's sexy, she must be dumb.
— She invited the sexual abuse. It was her fault, and now she's spoiled forever.
— Her sexuality and her sexual needs make her look ridiculous.
— Men can't help themselves. They naturally get sexually ag-gressive if a woman acts like a whore.
— Any man who says that sex is not a high priority in a rela-tionship is lying. So remember, you have to be sexual to please him, but never just to please yourself.
— A woman's sexual needs drain the man's vital energies. That's why athletes have to refrain from sex before compe-titions.
— Women must supply sexual energy for the cult leaders or for their gurus. It's their duty and an honor.

### Not All Inner Patriarchs Are Alike

*Please remember that Inner Patriarchs are not all alike! They do have their differences, and some are less negative than others in this, or other, areas.* These statements, however, do give a general picture of their values. Many of these views are such an integral part of our cul-ture that they seem quite ordinary and sensible—for instance, the disgust for menstrual blood. A bleeding wound is not seen as dis-gusting—frightening or messy perhaps, but not revolting. For most women, however, menstrual blood is a source of shame and disgust.

I remember being present in a roomful of women who gasped with a single breath as Danielle told us of an act that was, for her, an affirmation of her basic female nature. She told us how she had always been deeply ashamed of her menstrual blood. Her mother had taught her that this blood and her sexuality were disgusting and should be hidden. As she grew older, Danielle decided that she wanted to be more accepting of herself. One of the areas she wanted to heal was this sexual wounding and shame. She learned about sexuality and menstruation in other cultures and, one day when she was menstruating at the time of the full moon, she went outdoors into the forest and allowed her blood to flow into the Earth. She felt free and whole, no longer ashamed.

The Inner Patriarchs of our group were horrified and gasped, even though this was definitely not the "politically correct" way for us to react. Then, after a moment's hesitation in which we looked around us and saw that there were only women present, there was a feeling of relief and excitement. This feeling built until someone shouted her support. The group then broke into a spontaneous round of exuberant applause and jubilant shouting.

It was as though Danielle had reclaimed something important for all of us. It seemed to me as if the Inner Patriarchs of the women in this group, for a few moments at least, had lost their collective grips on this particular aspect of female sexuality. It felt as though a dull, familiar weight had been lifted, and a great surge of energy lifted the group. It was as if we had suddenly been given a great source of power that we could share with men and use in partnership with them. It was so very different from the usual feeling transmitted by our Inner Patriarchs that our sexuality is either a time bomb waiting to go off, which will do great damage, or something shameful that makes us inferior to men.

### So That's What Was Happening!

Sumie came up to speak with me after one of the lectures I gave on the Inner Patriarch. She said that she had just realized what had happened to her about 17 years earlier. This was an incident that had really puzzled her, and my description of the Inner Patriarch explained the mystery. Now the incident made complete sense. She could see that this was an incident during which her Inner Patriarch had emerged from the shadows, taken command, and with great passion, had made his feelings known. At that time, Sumie was a follower of an Indian guru who believed in ecstatic self-expression. She joined one of the most powerful of the encounter groups led by one of his star group leaders. The group met in one of the "therapy chambers" and were clad only in "Longies," small wraparound pieces of material.

One of the girls in the group started to become very sensual in her behavior. She moved like a snake as she writhed around the group leader; she purred like a cat; she put her head on his knee; and, during all this time, she seemed to be enjoying herself very much. The group leader was caressing her hair.

Sumie found herself getting more and more angry. Her fury built to a peak as she got up, took off her own Longie, and completely covered this "snake" with the cloth. This left Sumie totally un-clothed. Sumie was surprised to find herself doing this because she was extremely uncomfortable about being naked in public. How-ever, in this situation, her own intense discomfort was less im-portant than the need to have the overt sexuality of the "snake" covered. Now, 17 years later, Sumie realized that it was her own Inner Patriarch that could not permit the girl to behave in this fash-ion. Sumie was following his dictates, just like the nurse in Claire's dream had been following the dictates of *her* Inner Patriarch.

The group leader, realizing that this sensuous girl was acting out a disowned self for Sumie, explained that she needed to reclaim her own "snake." She followed this advice and took up Oriental (belly) dancing. Slowly she learned to enjoy the movements, allowing this snakelike feeling to move through her body as she danced. But even though she became very proficient at this kind of dancing and actually became a dance teacher, Sumie could not truly enjoy her-self. The form was correct and it looked good, but it was technique without meaning. No matter what she did to change her attitude, there was a feeling underneath that this was not right.

Now, many years later, it all became clear. Sumie's behavior had changed, but her Inner Patriarch had never been made a part of this process. He was still operating in her unconsciously, and he had never stopped telling her that this was shameful, that a woman should never move in this way. Like many other Inner Patriarchs I've met, a woman's sexuality was not acceptable to him.

Months later, I had the opportunity to talk with Sumie's Inner Patriarch, and this is what he said:

*Sidra:* It seems as though you have some feelings about Sumie's oriental dancing. What are they?

*Inner Patriarch:* The way she moves is absolutely disgusting, and I don't like it when she dances. I wish that she would stop it. She's too old.

*Sidra:* But what about when she was younger?

*Inner Patriarch:* I didn't like it then either. I don't think that a decent woman should behave that way. It's too sexual [wrinkling up his nose as though he smelled something dreadful].

*Sidra:* Tell me, what is your view of Sumie and her sexuality?

*Inner Patriarch:* Frankly, I think she's disgusting, and the less said about her sexuality, the better. I think her body is disgusting, her juices and her odors are disgusting, and it makes me sick just to think about anything having to do with her "down there" [pointing to the lower part of the torso].

And while we're discussing this, I don't like the fact that she needs sex. She should be ashamed of herself for that, and I'm glad to say that she is! If I had my way, she would be celibate. The only kind of woman that I admire is the one who is not interested in sex at all. I think that is much more attractive. I agree with her husband. I don't think sex is important, and I think that she should leave him alone. I think that it's humiliating when she approaches him and he's not interested. In my opinion, she acts like a whore.

*Sidra:* How does she act like a whore?

*Inner Patriarch:* First of all, she's too aggressive about sex with her husband. It just isn't right. The man should be the one to make the first move. It's bad—very, very bad—when the woman has sexual needs and she makes the first move.

Also, she dresses like a whore. I don't like bright colors, soft fabrics, flowing clothes, or anything that attracts attention. I would like to see her wearing pants, plain colors, and tailored things, more like a man. Her hair should be short and plain. Nothing provocative. Nobody should ever notice her. Nobody should ever think that she is a sexual person or that she has sexual needs.

*Sidra:* So you think that she would be better off if she had nothing at all to do with sex?

*Inner Patriarch:* Definitely.

*Sidra:* Would you feel the same way if she were a man? Do you think that a man is better off if he does not think about sex?

*Inner Patriarch:* A man is different. It's okay for a man to think about sex.

The intense negative feelings and powerful judgments of Sumie's Inner Patriarch are not unusual. I have heard many similar comments. *It's easy to see how the Inner Patriarch's humiliating comments shamed Sumie and prevented her from enjoying her own sexuality and sensuality. This shame is excruciatingly painful for many,*

71

*many women. In contrast, men are permitted, or even encouraged, in their sexuality.*

This might be a good time to think about your own Inner Patriarch's comments about sexuality. As you do so, check for this double standard. See how he would feel if the subject of his comments was a man rather than a woman. It's fascinating to discover how differently the Inner Patriarch reacts to a man's sexuality.

### The Difference Between a Woman's and a Man's Sexuality

*Most Inner Patriarchs (like Sumie's) view male and female sexuality differently. They look at a man's sexuality as a sign of his power. The more sexual he is, the more virile he is, and the more manly or powerful he is perceived to be. A woman's need for sexual contact, on the other hand, is seen as a problem. It can lead to all sorts of trouble, as well as to serious humiliation.*

Nan's father, a strong patriarchal type, was quick to encourage his sons when, at puberty, they began to show evidence of sexual interest. This meant that they were now men. His reaction to Nan, however, was quite different. Nan had been her Dad's special pal until puberty. They did everything together. They worked on the farm, and he loved to spend hours talking to her.

When Nan began to be attractive, her father withdrew from her as though in horror. He spoke to her about her blossoming sexuality, letting her know that he found it disgusting. His violent reaction toward her womanhood—and, we would expect, his horror at his own sexual reactions to her—caused her to totally deny her own sexual feelings. Nan's Inner Patriarch took over the disgust of her father and directed it against herself, her body, and her sexuality. The safest thing to do was to deny that she was a sexual person at all. As she grew older, she was literally unable to feel pleasurable sensations in her body.

Many years later when I spoke with her Inner Patriarch, Nan first heard his harsh judgments of her as a woman. But later, as we encouraged him to talk more about this subject, she heard his terror about her sexuality and his fear that she might lose control over herself and her actions. He was afraid that uncontrolled sexuality might ruin her life. He was even able to see how he needed to squelch her sexuality in order to keep her safe from her father.

Many women, especially those who have been close to their fathers, have had the experience of losing them when they reach puberty. Some, like Nan's father, are outspoken. These fathers tell their daughters that their sexuality is unacceptable. They make statements that the Inner Patriarch is happy to add to his collection. Other fathers withdraw suddenly, and their daughters are left to ponder the reasons why. Usually their Inner Patriarchs figure out that it has something to do with sexuality.

The mothers, of course, must teach their daughters something about the real dangers of their blooming sexuality. Often they do so by passing on the teachings and attitudes of their own Inner Patriarchs. If the mother does not teach her daughter some of this material, her daughter will not know about setting socially appropriate boundaries on her sexuality. She might well put herself in dangerous or, at the very least, unpleasant situations. It is also quite likely that she will be censured by the outside world. This is one of those areas where the Inner Patriarch has some valid concerns. However, I must note that his negative approach needs to be balanced by an appreciation of the positive aspects of female sexuality.

There is still what we used to call "a double standard" in our culture, a different set of rules by which men's and women's sexual behaviors are judged. The Inner Patriarch, with his own double standard, will alert the daughter to this. Unfortunately, these attitudes continue to uphold that same set of standards and keep women victims of them.

### The Inner Patriarch Deals Differently with Males and Females on the Issues of Sexual Provocation

If a female flirts with a male and he pursues her actively, her Inner Patriarch makes her feel guilty and says that she led him on, that his persistence must in some way be her fault. There is no possibility that he might have read her signals wrong. *Basically, Inner Patriarchs make women feel responsible for men's erections!*

Conversely, if a man flirts with a woman and she pursues him actively, her Inner Patriarch and the people around her let her know that she's a fool. If she claims that he flirted with her and led her on, she is told that she read the signs all wrong. The man is not in any way responsible for her attraction or her sexual interest. If he is at his most negative, the Inner Patriarch, and most likely the Outer Patriarchs as well, will mock her for this behavior.

There is a similar treatment of the transference/counter transference relationship in psychotherapy. When a female client becomes obsessed with her male therapist, cannot stop thinking about him and craves a sexual relationship, this is treated as fairly normal behavior. This is just a phase of therapy that many patients experience. It is to be expected and can even be vaguely amusing. The Inner Patriarch smilingly observes: "That's just what women are like in therapy. They fall in love with their therapists. All of them do it."

However, if a male patient becomes obsessed with his female therapist, cannot stop thinking about her and craves a sexual relationship, there is often a suspicion that the therapist has been acting seductively. This is not always seen as just a phase of therapy that all patients experience. Rather than accepting this as part of the natural course of events, the Inner Patriarch is likely to wonder: "What has the therapist done to provoke these sexual feelings, this intense sexual transference?"

## The Inner Patriarch Supports the Outer Patriarchy

This shows us how the attitude of the woman's Inner Patriarch's towards women's sexuality supports the generally negative attitudes held by our culture. The following excerpt from a conversation with Janet's very articulate Inner Patriarch gives a feeling of how this happens.

> *Janet's Inner Patriarch:* I want to talk about her sexuality. She's a slut. I'd rather see her be a weak child in relation to a man and to everyone else in the world than to own that [sexual] energy. It's dirty, it's dangerous, and I'm concerned for her about that. But basically it's nothing that anyone of importance would respect. Even the man she's doing it with.
>
> Her father told her that anybody who did stuff like that would be a slut, and I agree. I think that female genitalia is disgusting. It makes no sense to me whatsoever. I mean, with a penis, you can see it, you know what it's shaped like, it's there. Female genitalia—it's just very confusing to me, and I don't like what it does to men. I think that women should keep their legs crossed because when they open them, men go nuts, and I think it's the woman's responsibility to hold that energy back. I agree completely with religions that don't have women there [meaning in the place of worship] 'cause they would distract the men.
>
> If she lets out her sexuality at all, she should let it out like a little girl. That's okay. You can play with Daddy, you can flirt, but I do not like this powerful feeling that she can get. It confuses me, and I don't know what to do with it. I think it's best if she squashes it.

## The Inner Patriarch Makes Women Victims of the Judgments of Others

In this last example, Janet's Inner Patriarch is obviously very judgmental about her sexuality. He is quite ready to agree with anybody or any group that feels negative about female sexuality in general or Janet's in particular. This makes Janet a victim whenever the topic of sexuality is brought up. *If the Inner Patriarchs of women did not agree with the criticisms of the outer world, then the women would not be victims of these judgments.*

For instance, my Inner Patriarch does not have a rule about covering myself in order to make myself a proper woman. If someone I meet tells me to cover myself so that I will not be too seductive, this will not affect me emotionally, it will not make me feel ashamed. I can consider the value of the suggestion with objectivity. I might even decide to cover myself when visiting a Moslem country because I would be more comfortable and less likely to attract unwanted attention. I would, in this way, honor the customs of the place that I was visiting. But I would not feel evil or dirty if I did not do this. I would not automatically agree with the outer injunction because my Inner Patriarch does not whisper a matching comment in my ears. He has never told me that if I were a real woman I would want to cover myself.

Since my own Inner Patriarch does not care about these injunctions, I would not get particularly angry or rebellious either. Again, I would be objective, not emotional. My Inner Patriarch has not been trained to look at my clothes in this way, and I have no need to fight against this suggestion. I do not feel shamed, so I do not have to defend myself against the outer patriarchal demand.

This is one of the ways that our Inner Patriarchs work from the shadows. We hear the criticisms from the outside and assume that this is what is upsetting to us—that it is these outer criticisms that make us ashamed of our sexuality. However, it is only when our Inner Patriarchs, like Janet's, agree with the outer one, that we feel upset.

## Sensuality and Sexuality

*The Inner Patriarch does not distinguish between sexuality and sensuality. He confuses them and fears them both equally. As a result, he tries to keep women from experiencing their sensuality as well as their sexuality.* This was particularly apparent in the example of Sumie's Inner Patriarch and his reaction to the sensual snakelike movements of the girl in her encounter group. This girl was enjoying her sensuality to the fullest. She was not being sexual.

A woman's sensual enjoyment of herself, of being with others, or of her surroundings is suspect and sets off the Inner Patriarch's alarms. When she enjoys dancing freely or clothing herself in beautiful soft clothes or making herself look more beautiful just for the pleasure of it, he becomes judgmental; he reacts as though these were acts of sexual provocation.

The Inner Patriarch becomes critical when a woman experiences pleasant bodily sensations (not necessarily sexual), or as she luxuriates in sights, aromas, and sounds. He immediately links anything that hints of a sensual experience with sex and dismisses it as unacceptable. As women, it is important for us to become aware of this differentiation, to clarify this for our Inner Patriarchs, and to claim the right to our own sensual enjoyment of life.

## Ancient Wisdom and Modern Choice

*Our Inner Patriarchs constitute a major force that keeps us from having true choice about how we act in the world, about our power, our sensuality, and our sexuality. They keep us unquestioning daughters, adhering to (or rebelling against) the patriarchal edicts of an era that is passing. As we move toward change, we need to hear their voices and consider their suggestions. We must neither dismiss them automatically nor follow them automatically. As we will see in a later chapter, they bring with them a certain wisdom from millennia of experience. Even though the world that they came from is different from the one in which we now live, we need to incorporate their wisdom and their strength and make it a positive part of ourselves.*

# CHAPTER SIX

# THE INNER PATRIARCH, EMOTIONALITY, AND CONTROL

*Her challenge is the challenge that we all face in these coming years, how to balance the rules and structures that have been the legacy of the patriarchy with the creativity, the chaos and the movement that are part of the ever-changing universe in which we live.*

The Inner Patriarch is ambivalent about emotionality in women. He is one of the parts of us that admires logic, rationality, and self-control, which he sees as basically masculine traits. In contrast, he is one of the parts of us that fears emotionality, lack of focus, and reliance upon intuition, which he views as feminine traits. But women must be women, he reasons, and emotionality is part of the package. Nevertheless, this makes him uncomfortable.

Even though he must require us to be emotional in order to be true women, you will hear our Inner Patriarchs making comments such as:

— Women are too emotional and are always overreacting.
— You can never really understand a woman. I'm a thinker. Women can't think clearly.

— People are safer with men. In a time of need, they're clear-thinking and dependable. Women will not make good choices.

*Inner Patriarchs are unanimous in their denunciation of a woman's emotionality, and they emphasize her need for objectivity. They are just certain that the lack of an impersonal, objective approach to life makes a woman unsafe. However, they usually see this kind of cool objectivity as unfeminine.* The Inner Patriarchs I have met do not want a woman to wall herself off from others or to withdraw from warm, interpersonal contacts. They basically like women to be responsive to the needs and feelings of others. This is one of their rules of relationship. As the King said in *The King and I:* "It's a puzzlement!" A solution to this puzzlement is discussed in the fourth section of this book, but first let us examine the puzzlement or conflict itself.

This conflict—between the Inner Patriarch's need for a woman to be emotional and his fear that these emotions will lead to a lack of objectivity and control—creates a fair amount of confusion. Let us begin to sort out this confusion by looking at the Inner Patriarch's fears of lack of control or loss of boundaries.

### Out of Control

The following dream illustrates the very worst fears of the Inner Patriarch. He knows that too much emotionality and too much caring for others can be dangerous. In this dream, the dreamer is ruled by her emotions and has no boundaries between herself and others. She cannot gain control of the airplane (her movement through life) because she cannot be objective and attend to the business at hand.

*I dream that I am piloting an airplane and it is crashing. Although I'm the person responsible for this situation, I keep looking behind me at the passengers in the cabin. They are my husband, my children, and my friends. My energy is all directed towards them. I look at them and talk to them. I'm worrying about whether they are frightened or uncomfortable. I'm wondering what they might think of me and whether they disapprove of my letting the plane crash.*

*I want them to help me, and I know that they cannot; I'm the pilot, and nobody else can pilot this plane.*

### The "Catch-22" in This Scenario

*The Inner Patriarch believes that control—over the details of one's own life and over others' lives—is totally unfeminine and works to trivialize this need when it occurs in women. In men, this kind of control is admired by the Inner Patriarch.* In fact, he thinks that a man who has lost his power or his ability to control himself and others is useless, much as he thinks that an older woman who has outlived her youthful sexuality is useless.

When women feel the need for this kind of control, they usually try to disguise it. You can see this most frequently in women outside of the workplace. They make fun of themselves, of their need to be taken seriously, or of their desire to have others respect their needs for control.

Ginny is a very feminine woman in her early fifties. She grew up and raised her children before the feminist movement. She was a good wife and, because her husband was financially undisciplined, she learned bookkeeping and became the bookkeeper for his business. In this way, she was able to bring order and discipline into their lives, even though she clearly maintained a subservient place. After the marriage broke up, she became Controller for a major company. She was entirely self-taught.

She made the most of her traditionally masculine abilities to focus, to discipline herself, to determine a fair price, to demand money that was owed, and to control the flow of money. All this, however, was under the aegis of men. She performed this task as an employee of men, and she did it very successfully.

In later years, however, Ginny was unable to apply these skills to her own business. When she finally remembered that she had the skills necessary to take care of her own financial matters, she began to do so again, but her Inner Patriarch was not very happy with her. So she laughed apologetically and spoke to others about "Barbara the Bookkeeper" who took care of her money matters. When she realized how she had trivialized this very powerful and supportive energy, she began to look at it as a part of her heritage, a trait passed down from her grandfather to her father and then to her. She embraced it as a basically masculine self, and no longer made any apologies. She was free to use it in all its power.

Her Inner Patriarch had basically emasculated Ginny, depriving her of this very important part of her heritage, a power that has traditionally been viewed as masculine in our patriarchal society. *Claiming this part of her heritage was an inside job. No man on the outside could give her this power that had been denied her by the man within!* When she finally took this power comfortably and consciously, Ginny's Inner Patriarch was delighted to see that she had not lost her femininity. He then stopped criticizing her and began to support her, contributing his energies to providing even more of the authority and self-confidence that she needed for success in the world.

### The Double Standard for Self-Discipline

The Inner Patriarch has a double standard, but he operates similarly in women of all sexual preferences. I have heard the same kinds of comments from the Inner Patriarchs of gay, bisexual, and straight women. Let us see how Birgit's Inner Patriarch felt about her.

Birgit had been married for many years and had a daughter whom she loved very much. She loved her husband, too, but the sexual passion in their relationship died fairly early in their marriage. For the past several years Birgit had been involved in a passionate love affair with another woman.

Although Birgit wanted nothing more than to end her marriage and live with her lover, she controlled her desires and disciplined herself. She felt that this would be too upsetting to her husband and her daughter, and she did not wish to do them any harm. There was a voice inside her, however, that sounded quite angry with this decision. When I spoke with this self, I discovered that it was her Inner Patriarch. I spent some time talking with him about Birgit and her dilemma.

Birgit's Inner Patriarch was appalled about her sexual involvement with a woman, and this disapproval, which was expressed only at an unconscious level, caused her much conscious pain and guilt. He told me that he was very angry about her sexuality, which he felt was dominating her life and might ruin her own family and her lover's as well. When I pointed out how cautious and dependable Birgit had been, her Inner Patriarch arrogantly dismissed anything responsible that she had done during her marriage. He did not give her any credit for her remarkable financial and emotional contributions to the stability of the household. When I questioned him about this, he admitted that had she been a man he would have admired her professional expertise and financial success, but belonging to a woman, they did not deserve any praise. Despite much evidence to the contrary, he still felt that Birgit was basically driven by her emotions and was out of control.

Then I questioned Birgit's Inner Patriarch about the fact that she had sacrificed her own desires for the well-being of the family. She had contained her affair so that it would not interfere at home. Her Inner Patriarch was furious with her. He pointed out that she was being deceitful, just like a woman. He felt that she should be honest about her feelings and bring everything out in the open. I asked him what would happen if she did this. He admitted that everyone would get very upset and there might be serious problems for the family, but he felt that Birgit's only honest course of action was to break up the family and go to live with her lover. Of course, if she did as he asked, her actions would be quite damaging to the family, and this would prove that she was out of control and a very selfish person.

I then reversed the scenario. I asked Birgit's Inner Patriarch what he would say about a man in a similar situation, a man who had been having an affair with a woman he loved very much. This hypothetical man, like Birgit, had been confining the meetings with his girlfriend to one afternoon a week. I asked the Inner Patriarch, "What would you say about this man if he did not tell his spouse about his affair but carried the pain and the conflict by himself so that he would not upset her and create family problems?"

The Inner Patriarch beamed with satisfaction: "Now there is a man I would admire. He is sacrificing himself by not spending too much time with his girlfriend. He is not selfishly disrupting his family in order to live with her. He is being responsible and carrying all the pain and tension by himself in order to spare his family. Yes, indeed, that would be a very good man." There was no mention of uncontrolled feelings, unbridled dangerous sexuality, or dishonesty.

There are many similar examples of the Inner Patriarch's double standard. His differing requirements for men and women, especially when it comes to this area of emotions and emotional control, can be very confusing and upsetting for us as women. Let us examine this further.

### The Inner Patriarch and the Artist's Intensity

The Inner Patriarch has different rules for women and men about emotional intensity in creativity. This is quite similar to the double standard he has for sexuality and for power. If a man produces artistic works that are intense, emotional, and powerful, this is fine. If a woman does so, she is behaving inappropriately. The Inner Patriarch wants the woman writer, artist, or musician to temper her passions and to show them to the world only after they have been refined. This was beautifully demonstrated by Penelope's Inner Patriarch.

Penelope, a very attractive soft, feminine woman, was an accomplished artist, as was her mother before her. She had always earned her living as an artist and, at this point in her life, Penelope was in the midst of evolving a new style. But something was blocking her and keeping her from moving forward. As we delved into this area, we discovered that this blockage was Penelope's Inner Patriarch. As I talked with this Inner Patriarch, he expressed his fears about her intensity, her emotionality, and about a possible loss of control. Let us listen to this Inner Patriarch's concerns in his own words:

> *Sidra:* It sounds as though you have some objections to Penelope's new work.
>
> *Inner Patriarch:* I most certainly do! It's outrageous. The colors are too intense, and the content is shocking. It's not anything you would want to hang in your house. It's far too powerful and exciting. The whole thing is just too intense.
>
> Look here. I don't want her having feelings that are intense like that, and I certainly don't want her to let others know that she feels them.
>
> *Sidra:* You don't? Why not?
>
> *Inner Patriarch:* Of course I don't. Look [in an exasperated voice], I want her to have a relationship. It's very important to me that she has a man in her life, and I ask you, I ask you, just think about it: "What kind of man

would want a woman who would paint something like this?" [points to the photos of the new work with great disdain].

What would you think about a man who could love a woman who had intense feelings like these? Don't you think that if she did find one who could tolerate this that he would have to be very strange?

*Sidra:* You're pretty upset about this, aren't you?

*Inner Patriarch:* Definitely. This stuff is just too strong. It's too much of a statement. She should be more circumspect and gentle. It's just not womanly. A woman shouldn't have those images and, if she does, she should hide them. I'm ashamed of her and of how people will react in horror. You saw her other work [work that is delicate, flowing and very detailed]. Now that's the way a woman should paint. Besides, no real artist paints like this.

*Sidra:* But the German Expressionists did work that looked a little like this.

*Inner Patriarch:* Yes, I guess they did. But they were men.

*Sidra:* How would you feel about this work if Penelope were a man? Would you have a man hide this kind of painting?

*Inner Patriarch:* Of course not! [with enthusiasm]. I'd tell him to display it. I'm sure it would sell. It's really quite powerful. A man could make a lot of money with this kind of work.

*Sidra:* What could Penelope do to make you feel better about this new style?

*Inner Patriarch:* I'd have her work on it until she developed something that combined her old style, you know, the delicate fine detailed work that she showed you, with this new intensity. If she could bring the two together, that would be okay. People would not be so upset, and she would look more like a normal, feminine woman!

We can see how the Inner Patriarch can severely inhibit creativity in women by declaring some areas off-limits to women and available only to men. Here, in directly asking the Inner Patriarch about his concerns, we were able to give Penelope a new look at what was happening. She was able to move beyond the dualistic thinking of the Inner Patriarch.

As she thought about the comments of her Inner Patriarch, Penelope realized that she, too, enjoyed some of her previous work and that she did want to keep some of the discipline and grace of her original style. But it was time to add to this the excitement of her passion. She looked forward to the challenge of integrating the opposites of disciplined form and expressionistic passion. *In a way, her challenge is that which we all face in these coming years: how to balance the rules and structures that have been the legacy of the patriarchy with the creativity, the chaos and the movement that are part of the ever-changing universe in which we live.*

# WHERE HAVE WE BEEN?

*The Ways in Which
We Have Dealt with the
Inner Patriarch in the Past*

# CHAPTER SEVEN

# GOOD GIRL/BAD GIRL

*There was a little girl who had a little curl right
in the middle of her forehead, and when she was
good, she was very, very good, and when she
was bad, she was horrid.*

— Nursery rhyme

You are probably familiar with this old nursery rhyme. It's certainly one that I heard when I was growing up and, I blushingly admit, one that I passed on to my own daughters. It never occurred to me that I was passing on the injunctions of my own Inner Patriarch! It never occurred to me that this notion of good behavior was limited to us as "girls" and that I'd never think of saying this to a son, even if I *could* figure out how to make the rhyme work properly. *The Inner Patriarch is indeed like the air we breathe; we do not even notice it.*

What I've noticed over the years, however, is that we as women have learned to deal with our Inner Patriarchs in a number of ways. As I have said, *the Inner Patriarch is like a father within us, and we each react to him differently. Until recently, there have been two major patterns of reaction. Some women react to the comments of the Inner Patriarch as a good daughter and assume the role of the "good girl." Others rebel against this inner father and live the life of the rebel daughter or "bad girl."*

This good girl/bad girl dichotomy was beautifully illustrated by an experiment done by a women's group. This group knew that

91

their Inner Patriarchs expected them to defer to men, to literally step aside if a man approached them. They agreed to try to walk down the street and not swerve to the side when a man approached from the opposite direction. However, when the moment came, they found that they simply could not keep walking straight ahead. Instead, most of them became uncomfortable, then stepped aside and became compliant daughters. The few who did not defer to the men became angry and rebellious. The only way they could find the strength to move against the wishes of their Inner Patriarchs was to get angry and fight. Not a single woman was able to remain on her own path with the conviction that she was entitled to do so!

Since the rise of feminist consciousness, I have noted a fascinating new pattern emerge that is neither "good daughter" nor "bad daughter." More and more frequently, women are simply avoiding areas in which they will be subjected to the rules, exhortations, and judgments of this Inner Patriarch.

### The Good Daughter

The classical Good Daughter knows the rules and expectations of the outer patriarchy, and for her survival she is finely tuned in to the voice of her own Inner Patriarch. She listens to these rules, and she behaves accordingly. *She knows how to live in a man's world without making trouble for herself or for the men around her. It is quite possible for her to achieve success both personally and professionally, but she does this in an "appropriate" fashion.*

Marnie was a typical Good Daughter. She worked hard at school and followed all the rules. She was a high achiever and did very well on her examinations and written assignments. Marnie was careful about her image, however, and she never spoke up in class if there were males present. Her mother, passing on the rules of her own Inner Patriarch, had taught Marnie when she was quite young not to be too clever when there were males around. This would make them uncomfortable, and that would not do. One should never make a male uncomfortable with your expertise, power, or intelligence; it was just not done.

Marnie truly wanted to be a good person and to please her mother. She also wanted to be accepted by others and hoped to get married some day. She saw many women who were successful but alone, and she did not wish to be one of them. Her mother was married and obviously knew how to be attractive to men. So Marnie listened to her mother's teaching and was extremely cautious about showing her own intelligence or power. By the time she reached adolescence, Marnie did not have to be reminded about anything; her own Inner Patriarch knew the rules and would automatically rein her in whenever it seemed as though Marnie might move beyond the realm of good daughter and demand too much attention, power, or respect.

Actually Marnie's Inner Patriarch did know how to "handle" men. He coached her in how to be a good girl, in manipulation, and in all sorts of "womanly wiles." He told her how men felt and what they expected, and she was able to behave accordingly. She knew the rules of the game and followed them. Although Marnie lived life as a good daughter, she did not feel particularly exploited. After all, the rules were just the rules. When Marnie was with men, they felt good about themselves and they liked her. Interactions were comfortable, nonconfrontational, and smooth.

### The Victim Daughter

Sometimes, however, things do not work out as well for women who try to be good daughters as they did for Marnie. Nan tried very hard to be a good daughter, but she had a simply dreadful Inner Patriarch. He, like both her father and her mother, thought that women were inferior to men in every way. Her Inner Patriarch became particularly vicious whenever Nan was in a relationship. At these times, he would team up with another critical self, Nan's

Inner Critic, to point out her shortcomings and make her wrong about everything all of the time. No matter how she tried to be a good daughter, she failed. Everything she did was wrong.

Nan could not defend herself against these attacks from within, so instead of becoming the good daughter to the Inner Patriarch, she became the victim daughter, and this Victim Daughter became her primary self. Unfortunately, this meant that she became a victim daughter to everyone she met, but this was the case particularly in her relationships to men. After all, her Inner Patriarch assured her, they were always right.

As she listened to the negative comments within, Nan would feel terribly insecure about herself and wrong about everything she did. She became particularly apologetic and self-deprecating in her relationship with the man in her life. She was constantly making negative comments about herself, hoping that, because he loved her, he would reassure her.

Nan would say things such as:

"Oh, God, how could I be so stupid?"
"Don't I look awful?"
"That's just like me to forget!"
"I never could do math."
"Computers confuse me."
"I'm sorry I made such a mess of things."

Now Nan was not really that incompetent. Knowing this, her boyfriends invariably tried to reassure her for a while, almost like good fathers telling her that she was really quite bright and did a good job. However, sooner or later, the boyfriends would become irritated and angry. They invariably began to look at her just like her Inner Patriarch did and saw the same "faults" he pointed out to them. Each boyfriend finally behaved the way Nan's father did, like a negative patriarch who had no respect for women and who made devaluing comments to her that echoed the ones of the patriarch within her. Until Nan can deal effectively with her own Inner Patriarch, she will always be a victim of his comments and will even create outer patriarchs in this way. She will tend to attract people who support the beliefs and feelings held by her own Inner Patriarch. In addition, her own behavior, which is directed by her Inner Patriarch, will bring out the Patriarch in others.

### The Rebel Daughter

Jane, in contrast to Marnie, was always on the lookout for exploitation and inequities. She was extremely sensitive to manipulation and to any practices that gave an unfair advantage to males. Jane's father had been a patriarchal man with all the accompanying advantages and disadvantages. Her father was extremely responsible and dependable. He felt that he, as the head of the household, was the only person in the family capable of making good decisions. He was strong and, when necessary, self-sacrificing. He tried to protect his family from the pressures and dangers of the world outside their home. In return, he expected to be admired, obeyed, and to retain complete control over all important family decisions.

When she heard the voice of her own Inner Patriarch urging her to act like a woman, to defer to a man, or to accept a secondary role, Jane was reminded of her father. She immediately became rebellious and pushed beyond his objections. *No matter what it was that her Inner Patriarch said, Jane fought it like a petulant child. She actually had no more choice in dealing with her Inner Patriarch than Marnie had. The only difference was that Marnie automatically acquiesced, and Jane automatically rebelled. Neither was free to really make her own choices.*

I remember when one of my daughters was going through a rebellious period—she was two years old at the time—and she simply had to say no to whatever it was I said. I could not resist enticing her with something I knew she wanted to see if she would continue to rebel. So I suggested that we go out for ice cream, something she dearly loved to do. Since she was living her life as a rebellious daughter, she simply had to say no to this offer just as she had to everything else.

It's important to note that Jane was only aware of the fact that she was rebelling against the outer patriarchal system, something she could talk about with much accurate information, true authority, and intense passion. In actuality, she was rebelling not only against the outer patriarchy, but against her own Inner Patriarch as well. She was aware of the success or failure of her encounters with the outer patriarchs of the world, but she knew nothing about the encounters with the Shadow King that lived inside, her own Inner Patriarch.

### Avoiding the Inner Patriarch's Territory

In years gone by, there have always been a few women who have chosen to elude their Inner Patriarchs by avoiding the major territory that they rule, that of relationships and marriage. Many have been writers who have written about their experiences. One of these women was Louisa May Alcott, who spoke about the impossibility of a woman truly living her own life if she was married to a man, because she would then have to put her needs aside and cater to his. Now, we could speculate that she might have found a man who would not require this sacrifice. But even if she had met a man who treated her as an equal, Alcott would still have to deal with the demands of her own Inner Patriarch, the one who was trained by her mother. It was the rule of this Inner Patriarch that once you are married, you belonged to your husband totally, and everything that you had was to be used for his benefit. To do otherwise would mean that she was not a good wife!

Alcott knew about the demands of the Inner Patriarch and about the good daughters who follow his rules of relationship. Her novel, *Little Women*, beautifully portrayed the various aspects of the archetypal good daughter. There is Meg, the loving, motherly good daughter; Jo, the ever-responsible, sturdy, creative good daughter; Beth, the gentle, spiritual good daughter; and Amy the flirtatious, seductive good daughter. I would like to point out that Mrs. March, the girls' mother, is also a good daughter. She is the ever-loyal, uncomplaining, cheerful good girl who follows the rules as she supports her husband and adores him no matter what he does. None of the little women (and women, as we know, are supposed to be "little" and not "big" according to our Inner Patriarchs) has any real power or real choice in life. None of them can take her life into her own hands, independent of the men around her. But they certainly do have a sweet and a wonderful life, even in times of adversity!

In recent years, more and more women have avoided the Inner Patriarch's demands by avoiding committed, monogamous relationships. Sadly enough, they do not always realize that it is their own Inner Patriarch who dictates this choice. Instead, they project his demands upon the men in their lives and see these demands as coming from them.

This is the way it works: Lynette's Inner Patriarch says that it is her task to clear the dinner table nightly. Instead of seeing this as a demand of her Inner Patriarch, Lynette projects this demand on to her boyfriend, Bob, much as a movie projector projects an image on to a movie screen. Lynette just *knows* that Bob expects her to clear the table when they finish eating. In her mind, he, not her own Inner Patriarch, is the source of these demands.

Lynette considers Bob's "demands" an insult to her dignity and her sense of equality, and she resents him for his expectations. Nonetheless, she resentfully clears the dinner table and does the dishes every night. She never asks Bob how he feels about this because her Inner Patriarch thinks that he always knows how men feel and what they expect. Lynette's Inner Patriarch knows that however much a man might protest, he basically wants his dinner dishes cleared and washed. (Please note here that, although their batting averages are good, Inner Patriarchs' readings of these situations are not always perfect.)

Now Lynette sees herself as a sophisticated women. She believes in the equality of the sexes and is quite clear that she does not want to be trapped by the expectations of a man. What she does not realize is that many of these expectations arise within herself, like a traitor waiting to collaborate with the outer enemy. Her Inner Patriarch makes statements such as: "If you get married, your husband is going to want you to put his needs first." Or: "Whatever they say to you when they're courting, men want to be superior to you." Or: "There is no way to keep your power if you marry." Lynette thinks these are truisms and sees all men as potential despots.

With the help of her Inner Patriarch, Lynette reads all the subtle signs that seem to support his beliefs. She is not reacting to Bob, the man outside, but to her Inner Patriarch's view of him. She continues to meet all these perceived expectations because her Inner Patriarch tells her that this is what Bob really wants despite what he says. This leads to trouble in the relationship.

Bob takes pains to be politically correct in his views and behavior. He has worked hard to rid himself of his patriarchal expectations. He wants equality in his marriage. That is one of the characteristics that Lynnette found so appealing about him. But, despite this, Bob, like all other men, still has a patriarchal voice within him. If Lynnette continues to be dominated by her own Inner Patriarch, this patriarchal voice in Bob will sooner or later come to life. When Bob's Patriarch becomes active, he does, in fact, expect Lynette to follow the traditional rules of wifely behavior. At that point, her Inner Patriarch is right; Bob does want her to be a good girl and so she is.

Eventually Lynette tires of Bob and all his "male chauvinist" requirements of her. The sad ending to this tale is that she leaves Bob without ever having discovered his real feelings and expectations and without having her own role in this drama become conscious for her. It was all played out in the shadows of her unconscious. If she had known about her Inner Patriarch, the relationship might well have taken an entirely different course. The Inner Patriarch's interpretations of a man's expectations in a relationship and the tendency of the woman to become either a good daughter or a rebellious daughter causes serious difficulties. Let's look at another example of how this plays out in relationship.

Marianne, a woman in her late sixties, observed me while I spoke to the Inner Patriarch of Pam, a younger woman who had recently married. Although this new husband had been Pam's lover for quite some time, the marriage immediately brought the Inner Patriarch to the foreground with his rules on how a woman should treat a husband. These rules were strict and seemingly endless. To summarize, Pam was now responsible for her husband's physical, emotional, and spiritual well-being. If he did poorly at work, she was probably creating stress at home that accounted for this. If he gained weight, she was feeding him wrong. If he became ill, she was definitely doing something that was undermining his natural resistance.

Pam's Inner Patriarch also wanted to be sure that, since she was now married, she was a good wife and took care of wifely duties such as the laundry. Pam always worked full time and had never done these tasks before They had been shared equally when she and her new husband had been live-in partners. But marriage had changed all that, and now Pam was exhausted with all her new responsibilities and irritated with all of her husband's new "demands." Pam's new husband was the same person he had been before the marriage. Ironically, these changes that annoyed Pam so very much and made her new marriage so burdensome had been put into effect by Pam's Inner Patriarch without even consulting her husband.

Marianne was astounded as she listened to Pam's Inner Patriarch. Marianne had been married once many years before, but after her divorce, she avoided marriage. She had many lovers, and there was much excitement in her life, but she never permitted herself to become deeply involved in a committed, monogamous relationship. She refused to be trapped again by the needs of a man or subject to his demands! As she listened to Pam's Inner Patriarch, Marianne realized that the demands she perceived as coming from the men around her had actually been coming from the patriarch within her for the past 40 years! For all that time, she had been running away from a picture that she projected onto the men in her life, and she had never stopped long enough to see what was really there.

However, Marianne had been successful. She had avoided the criticisms and demands of her own Inner Patriarch. She did not play in his playground and therefore did not have to follow his rules. As long as she associated primarily with women and kept her relationships with heterosexual men fairly superficial, she was not faced with the humiliating commentary and the sexist demands of her Inner Patriarch. She had lived her life as a self-respecting, independent human being.

### You Do Not Have to Play

*We no longer have to be either good girls or bad girls in dealing with our Inner Patriarch. We do not have to become rebels or avoid relationships entirely in order to separate from our Inner Patriarch and his demands.*

In the following chapters, we will explore alternative ways of dealing with this pervasive and often difficult self. We will look at what he wants, what he fears, and what we can do to balance his power. We will learn to honor him, giving him the respect that is his due, and learn how we can limit the destructive aspects of his effects on our lives as women.

# THE INNER MATRIARCH

*The Inner Patriarch makes a woman ashamed,
apologetic, or defensive about being a woman.
In contrast, the Matriarch is proud of women.
She thinks that women are far superior to
men. She brings with her a respect for women
and for everything that has traditionally been associated with the feminine. She is neither impressed nor intimidated by men or by the
traditionally masculine ways of the world.*

There has always been a need to balance the power of the
Inner Patriarch, just as we as women have worked to balance the power of the outer patriarchy. There are two
major reasons for this. First of all, without this balance, the Inner
Patriarch runs our lives, keeping us in the role of daughter to the
men around us. If we can separate from his influence, we will be
in a position to be equal partners with the men in our lives. Secondly, the gifts that the Inner Patriarch brings with him are rationality, law, order, discipline, focus, productivity, competition,
control, the emphasis upon achievement, the mandate to protect
the weak, and the adherence to well-defined roles that give us a
predictable world. These gifts represent only one half of our legacy
as human beings. The other half of our gifts are carried by other
selves.

### The Inner Matriarch

There is a Matriarch in women, a voice that tries her best to balance the power of the Inner Patriarch and his set of values. I see this Matriarch as a primary self for women, a self that is conscious and one of our power voices. She comes forth, like a warrior, to protect us as women and to protect the traditionally feminine values that we carry. When a corresponding voice occurs in men, I call it the Inner Matriarch. Like the Inner Patriarch, she has a good side and a bad side.

The Matriarch is angry at the injustices and inequities that she sees in a world where men are valued more than women. She sees the dangers of extolling the traditionally masculine values and demeaning or trivializing the traditionally feminine ones. Her heart breaks for the young girls left to die in Asia because they are considered worthless. She personally mourns for each ten year old who is sold into sexual slavery, for girls who are genitally mutilated, and for women who have been denied even their most basic rights as human beings. She is infuriated by rape and usually demands castration as the only appropriate punishment for a man who refuses to accept responsibility for controlling his sexual impulses. She sees very little of value in men or their world.

*The Matriarch is a self in women who views her own gender as superior to men. She has a very negative opinion of men and traditionally male qualities. Since she does not echo the views of the dominant culture, she has not been as much of a problem for men as the Inner Patriarch has been for women. Recently, however, more and more men are suffering greatly from the cruelty of their own Inner Matriarchs and, I might add, from the cruelty of the Matriarchs of the women around them.*

This suffering has always been the fate of men who were raised by women who dislike males. A boy growing up in a household without a strong male presence to balance this negativity usually carries within himself a strong Inner Matriarch who disapproves of him and of his feelings and behaviors just because he is a male. As you can see, this is very similar to the Inner Patriarch's role in the lives of women.

Ron, for instance, was raised by his mother. His father had abandoned the family when the youngest child was born, leaving Ron's mother to raise three children on her own. Ron was the only male in the household for as long as he could remember. His mother and his sisters were always around, and his grandmother and his aunts helped out from time to time. His mother did have some boyfriends, but they were not really interested in him, so basically there were no men in Ron's life.

Ron grew up hearing the women in the household complain about how unfeeling, irresponsible, and cruel men were and how, if it weren't for women, the entire world would fall apart. These complaints became the litany of Ron's Inner Matriarch. She truly believed that men were bad, and she did not hesitate to let Ron know this. Since Ron was a male, he, of course, would be as bad as the rest of the men in the world unless he renounced all his manly characteristics. But if he listened to his Inner Matriarch and became more feminine, Ron would be judged negatively by the Inner Patriarch (his own and others') as too effeminate.

There is support for men like Ron in the dominant culture to ignore the voice of the Inner Matriarch. There is much encouragement for them to maintain their masculinity and to resist the judgments of the misguided females (or wimps) of the world, but this has little effect on the negative voice that lives within him. The Inner Matriarch, like the Inner Patriarch, will not be silenced so easily. This poses quite a dilemma. We could say that Ron and other men like him are living between a rock and a hard place.

In recent years, the power of the Matriarch has also been enhanced by a great deal of the "New Age" thinking and many of the feminist values. The matriarchal voice in both men and women is critical of power, aggression, competition, unfeeling sexuality, and exploitation. She values feelings, cooperation, the cycles of nature, love, family, and nurturing. She is usually at war with the Inner Patriarch, although there are times, as we will see in the following description of Margie, when they might both disapprove of the same behavior.

Margie is a writer and she works at home. She has hired an excellent baby-sitter so that her children will not be neglected when she must concentrate on her work. Margie has learned to ignore her children's cries when she has a deadline to meet. Margie remains in her home office and lets the baby-sitter take care of their needs even though she can hear them fussing in the next room. At these times, Margie's Matriarch says something like: "You are acting just like a man. That is bad. Do not forget that your children are the most important part of life. Don't neglect them in order to further your career. That is a sign of bad priorities. You will hurt them just like your father hurt you when you were less important than his work at the office! That is what is wrong with the world today."

Margie's Matriarch does not see the importance of focusing upon individual tasks, self-discipline, or success in the world. So, she joins forces with the Inner Patriarch, who believes that a woman's place is in the home, that she should dedicate herself to her husband's needs and the needs of her children. Both have the same demands for Margie. The difference between them is that Margie's Matriarch thinks that the focus on the family is more exalted than her professional life, and her Inner Patriarch feels that her professional life is basically more worthwhile than her focus on the family.

### A Voice in the Shadows

*Like the Inner Patriarch, the Inner Matriarch lives deep in the unconscious and does much of its harm in the shadows beyond our awareness. She makes men feel ashamed about themselves and their traditionally masculine traits. She makes women ashamed of themselves, too, if they think, act, or feel like a man. If it is traditionally masculine, it is bad.*

I have spoken to many Inner Matriarchs, and I have decided to use a single example, George's, because she is elegantly articulate as she gives her views of men, women, and the important things in life. As you listen to her speak, you will hear her gentleness and sadness. You will also hear her ambivalence and her emphasis upon the more traditionally feminine values. Finally, you can hear her generally negative view of men and of their world. She spoke thoughtfully, gently, and very slowly. Some Inner Matriarchs are more angry and militant, but this one was wistful and sad.

*Sidra:* I'd like to hear about your feelings concerning the place of women in the world today.

*Inner Matriarch:* You know that this world is not safe for women, particularly if you are in a male's body. It's not safe for me to be out in this world.

*Sidra:* Why is that?

*Inner Matriarch:* If I come out in the wrong places, I can get him into real trouble. Men don't like me at all. I used to be able to come out more in him. I was able to be sensitive, and there were certain women who really liked me. There are certain places where I can come out—when he is listening to somebody, when he's nurturing somebody, when he can be gentle.

I was able to come out when he was a young man and he became a Christian. Then my compassion and gentleness was accepted. Yes, and when he was an orderly in the hospital when he was about 19. Then he could be compassionate. I could be kind to the little old ladies and they loved it. But the older he gets, the less room there is for me. When he was a boy, I was okay, but not as a man.

*Sidra:* So when he was a boy, it was okay, but not as a man. When he grew up, he had to be a man, and he had to put you away. It's like that with girls, too. They are allowed to be more like boys until they reach puberty, and then they're told to act like women.

*Inner Matriarch:* Yes, that's right. I wish there was a place for me in his life, but I'm definitely a woman and I really love women.

*Sidra:* Is there any particular kind of woman whom you admire?

*Inner Matriarch:* The women I admire are really in touch with their sexuality, and they really enjoy it. I wish they would like me. I really enjoy their femininity, the way they enjoy their sexuality, the way women can give birth. I envy them that. I'm sorry that he can't have a baby. When I was young, I had a friend whose wife was pregnant, and I used to think how wonderful it would be if I could feel life inside of me and I could give birth like she did.

I've always really been sad that he's in a man's body. I envy that you were born in a woman's body [with real yearning]. They're so soft and gentle and compassionate. The way that women can be intimate, the secrets that they can share, the way they can get so very, very close.

*Sidra:* It sounds like it's a feeling—a flowing, sensuous, soft feeling.

*Inner Matriarch:* Right, and it's a bigness, too, that they have. And women get wounded for the right reasons. Women know what is important. Not like men.

*Sidra:* What would be important? What would a woman react to that a man might overlook?

*Inner Matriarch:* [sadly] Suffering, a person's suffering, would be a right reason, a wounding that didn't need to happen would be a right reason. A loss of life. None of those things that men do. Men are so shallow. Life, death, spirituality, feeling and intimacy. Feeling mostly.

*Sidra:* You said that men get concerned with things that aren't so important. What would these be?

*Inner Matriarch:* Winning! Men worry a lot about winning. Winning a tennis game. His dad, you know, he'd spend hours practicing to win a local competition and then get all upset about it if he didn't. Winning and competition, that's what men worry about. What is so important about winning and losing? They don't gain anything from winning or losing. I'm not opposed to playing games or competition, but it's the anger and the spending of resources, spending time away from their families and their homes. They spend time doing things that stroke their egos and that take away from loving and relating.

You know [getting a little louder and harsher], they let their little egos get in the way. So sometimes they're wrong. You know, when men are wrong, they get all defensive and then they hurt people. That's the problem.

*Sidra:* You mean that when men are hurting, they hurt others?

*Inner Matriarch:* Yes. So what if they're wrong? We're all wrong sometime. That's no excuse to hurt someone. Women are just much better than men. They don't do that.

*Sidra:* So you have a very strong injunction against hurting people.

*Inner Matriarch:* Yes, I would! I'm against hurting others, against causing pain.

*Sidra:* If it came to a choice between George getting hurt, or the other person getting hurt, physically or emotionally, do you have any rules about that?

*Inner Matriarch:* Not me, not really. I'm not a martyr or altruistic; I don't want to hurt anybody, but I don't want to get hurt. I can get angry and sometimes I can lash out. But somebody has to hurt me first before I will do that.

You know, if men are at war, and if you've got to kill or be killed, that's the way it is; that's sad. But that's not what I'm talking about. I'm talking about how a man needs to prove how good he is and how he hurts others by this. That should be just for boys. When a boy grows up, he should be a man and stop that. It's hollow and not important.

*Sidra:* So you would contain that need to compete just to prove that he's better than others. What other kinds of things would you contain?

*Inner Matriarch:* I would not contain it. I would probably just want to reach in there and cut it out, whatever it is, and throw it away, this thing that needs to dominate. Mostly it has to do with their lack of feeling.

When women are as shallow and catty and as cruel as men, then I think they are terrible. I used to think that all women were like me, but now I know that there are some women like men, and I don't like them at all. Conversely, there are some men like me, and I really like them.

*It is clear that the Inner Matriarch has strong opinions about what is important and what is not, independent of gender. She does not have a double standard like the Inner Patriarch, who admires some behavior in men (like self-assertion). The Inner Matriarch condemns the same behavior and values in both sexes.* She feels negative about most of what we have traditionally considered "masculine," finding this unacceptable in women as well as in men. Conversely, she values traditionally "feminine" values and behaviors, giving her approval of these in men as well as women.

## What Should We Do with Men?
## The Inner Matriarch's View

George's unconscious gave a beautiful picture of his Inner Matriarch's view of a man's place in the world. He dreamt that his mother lived in the main house with her children. She required his father to live in a separate structure, outside of this house. This structure was lower than the main house and set down into a large rectangular pit dug about 15 feet into the earth. It was a perfectly comfortable structure. The roof was covered with earth, and it looked a bit like a hunting lodge. His father would be comfortable living there. Thus, in George's dream, the man was completely separated from the women and the children.

With this picture of the exiled male in mind, I asked George's Inner Matriarch what she thought should be done with men. Her voice was harsher and more judgmental than it had been earlier, and this was the answer that she gave me:

> *Inner Matriarch:* Basically I think that men need to be out of the way. Out of the way of the home, the family, love, and nurturing. I don't need them to be in any unpleasant place, but I just like to keep them out of the house. If men would just keep out of our way, the world would be a better place.

111

*Sidra:* Are there any places that would be appropriate?

*Inner Matriarch:* I would really like it if George were in one of those hunting societies, and we could send the men off to hunt and we would take care of the kids and do all the important things [becoming quite patronizing]. Then they could come home at night and paint their faces and dance and do whatever they wanted to do, but they would not be involved in the really important things that we have to do to keep ourselves together.

*Sidra:* It sounds as though you feel it is a good idea to keep men out of the way in order to keep the civilization together.

*Inner Matriarch:* You bet! When they get into the home, they just fuck things up. They're just too hard and cruel, unfeeling and uncaring. At best, they're not there; at worst, they fuck up. Send them to the moose lodge and let them do their moose thing. I think it's really silly. Men are so shallow! We women are so deep!

Let me point out that it is the Inner Matriarch that has no use for men. She is only one of our selves. There are other selves that feel quite differently.

### The Castration of the Male

Just as the Inner Patriarch trivializes women and makes them feel dreadful about themselves, an Inner Matriarch makes a man feel uncomfortable about his masculinity. *Any testosterone-related behavior is severely judged. The Inner Matriarch shames a man for his natural aggression, sexuality, territoriality, or competition. She tries to quiet him and calm him, to focus all his energies upon feelings and nurturing. She points out that he cannot truly care for himself. She is only happy with a "good boy."* Unfortunately, as I've mentioned earlier, the Inner Patriarch has only scorn for the good boys of the world. This can make life very confusing for everyone!

The cruelty that co-exists with the compassion of the matriarchal voice was apparent in this dream of a young woman:

*I dreamt that I was in a large room with the women of my family. My mother, my grandmother, my great-grandmother, and all my aunts were with me. The older women were passing around a jar with something in it. Each woman looked carefully as she received it, and then passed it to the next one. When my turn came and I looked at the jar, I saw that it contained the genitals of my father.*

This castration is usually symbolic and subtle. We see it when the *Matriarchs mock men's behavior. They often talk about men as though they were all little boys.* They sound like George's Inner Matriarch did when she scornfully suggested that the men get together and go out hunting so that they would keep busy and out of the way. When a group of Matriarchs have the opportunity to speak, these are some of things you might hear them say:

— I think that women are basically stronger than men.
— All men are really little boys underneath.
— Men don't know about what is really important.
— Woman really know what is important.
— Men do not know how to feel.
— Men are always competing and showing off.
— Men need to be handled. If you know how to handle them properly, you can get whatever you want.
— It is the men who are responsible for the mess that this world is in.
— Men like to fight. If it were up to the women, there would be no wars.
— Men think with their penises.

— Women can tolerate much more discomfort than men. If men had to go through pregnancy and childbirth, there would be no children.
— Men don't really care what happens to others. They only pretend.
— Men are only interested in one thing [meaning sex].
— Men are cruel.
— Men are naturally competitive; only women know how to cooperate.
— I've never met a nurturing man.
— I don't trust men. They are all users.

The feeling tone of the Inner Matriarch often contrasts with the Inner Patriarch, who can become cold, quite angry, or judgmental. Her approach is likely to be condescending or scornful. In her negative aspect, she uses her knowledge of feelings and needs to manipulate a man and make him feel totally inadequate.

With a mocking look, the Inner Matriarch can shut a man out of the family warmth and closeness. He will feel like an abandoned child who cannot do anything right. She makes all his talents, his achievements, and his power unimportant and unimpressive and lets him know that, in her view, his accomplishments mean nothing.

### The Positive Aspects of the Matriarch

*The Matriarch helps to balance the Inner Patriarch in women. The Inner Patriarch makes a woman ashamed, apologetic, or defensive about being a woman. In contrast, the Matriarch is proud of women. She thinks that women are better than men. She brings with her the respect for women and for everything that has traditionally been associated with the feminine. She is not intimidated by men or the traditionally masculine ways of the world. In this way she gives women a sense of self-respect*

114

*and carves out a place for them, a place where they can be proud of themselves and their sex.*

Let's listen to the comments of Karen's Matriarch.

"Karen was raised by a very strong mother, and I'm very proud of her mother. Basically, I'm proud of her female lineage. I'm proud of her mother, her grandmother, and her great-grandmother. They may not have done anything out there in the world, but they were all powerful women. They held the families together and supported their men, who were actually weaker than the women, so that they could go out and make it in the world. I'll bet that if they had been born during these last 30 years, they would have gone on to become very powerful in the world—that is, if they really wanted to.

"Basically, I think that men are worthless without women. They all need somebody to take care of them because they don't know how to do that themselves, and it takes a strong woman to do that.

"As far as I'm concerned, a woman can make it on her own. She always has friends and family; she knows how to roll with the punches. She'll do what she has to do. Women have always been survivors, and they have the instincts and the deep knowledge of survivors. You know, men are a little like children. They don't know about their vulnerabilities and sensitivities. If they're not powerful or in charge, they don't know what to do. Women can be tough even when they're down, and I think that is real power.

"You know, women have a deep and a secret knowledge if they let themselves feel it. Women are attuned to the cycles of life. Their bodies and their rhythms are special. They have intuitive gifts that are astounding. I've read that they are healthier, that they live longer, and that they can withstand pain and fight infection better than males. Also, they can survive the loss of a spouse better than a man can. I think that women are amazing, totally amazing.

"I keep reminding her that men just don't have access to anything really important. My job is to tell Karen about this and to help her to get to her own deep knowing and feminine power. That's why I like her to read books about women and attend women's groups. Also, those activities make her proud to be a woman. I like her to appreciate everything about her womanliness. It's totally ridiculous to go around feeling disempowered or "less than" a man! Totally ridiculous."

We can see how this Matriarch helps Karen to balance the power of her Inner Patriarch. For Karen, or for any individual woman, it can counter his disparaging remarks and give her a real sense of pride in her female lineage. *Unfortunately, this is sometimes won at the price of devaluing the men in her life.* In this way, the Matriarch is just like the Inner Patriarch, and we can see that it brings both gifts and problems.

*In a broader sense, the Matriarch lets both men and women see the importance of the traditionally feminine values in life. The Matriarch protects the values of feelings, of home, of family, and of community. She safeguards the sanctity of the ordinary, and of the cycles of life that cannot be manipulated or changed no matter how much we learn.* The Matriarch values the well-being of the individual before that of the group. She places her feelings and love before anything else, especially abstract principles. She has her values and wishes to be with others who agree with them, even if this means that she must move away from the world of men in order to meet people who look at life as she does.

This chapter has given you a picture of the Matriarch and the ways in which her attributes, her values, and her power can provide some balance in our psyches. In the following section of this book, I would like to look at some other ways in which we can work creatively with the Patriarch that lives within each of us. Our goal is to balance the opposites represented by these two selves. As we do this, we move into a new way of being in the world that honors our full potential as human beings and allows men and women to partner one another with equality and dignity.

# A NEW PATH

# A New Path for Women

*In my dream I am carrying a large parcel of important women's "treasures." This must be delivered to a group where men and women work as partners in a new kind of partnership. But the way is precipitous and dangerous. There is no path. As I walk, my footing often gives way, and rocks slide out from beneath my feet. I must concentrate all my consciousness upon the moment, upon the placement of my feet at each step. I must relate to my body and to the earth. If not, I will not be able to complete my task.*

*Only men have passed this way before, and they conquered by will, by pushing beyond barriers, by brute force. They succeeded in reaching their goals, but they carried nothing of the feminine with them. I must reach the goal in a new way and, as I struggle towards it, I must not drop any of my female gifts.*

— Sidra Stone

What is this new way, and how can we move toward our goals, each of us carrying our own particular gifts? Up until now, most of us have relied upon more traditionally masculine strategies to accomplish this task. The Inner

Patriarch has helped us, both women and men, to succeed in a patriarchal, competitive world. This goal cannot be reached by us if we try to become pseudo-males, or work to prove that we as women are innately better than men by exalting the traditionally female or feminine. They can only be reached when we move beyond the male/female duality and realize we are all human beings. Each of us has a unique set of gifts to bring to the world, and whenever we divide these gifts by gender, racial, tribal, religious, or any other kind of divisive groupings, we undermine our ability to utilize them fully.

First we must realize that the Inner Patriarch is not our enemy. In fact, there are ways in which he protects and supports women. There are many times when his basic motivations are positive, even though the way he expresses them or puts them into action may look negative to us. Much of what I have described up until now has focused upon his negative impact upon us. I have shown how our self-image and our behavior is affected by his often negative messages.

The Inner Patriarch is just like any person we might meet in our lives. If we feel angry and resentful, if we are defensive and ready to fight, if our goal is to conquer him, he will fight back. And he is very, very strong! Not only does he have the power of his current observations, but he carries with him the values and judgments of the collective, the culture that surrounds us and that largely supports him.

Fighting the Inner Patriarch is not a good idea. We will not win. Giving in to his power and becoming a daughter to him is not a particularly good idea either. When we do that, we lose our power as women, and we do not make our unique contribution to the world in which we live. We abandon it to the men and then blame them for the results.

The Matriarch may make us feel better about ourselves. As we gather in groups with other women, as we talk with our friends and feel the camaraderie and the support of our sisters, as we negate the gifts of the men in our lives, we may get a taste of female superiority and power, but we are achieving this at the expense of the men in the world. Our sense of superiority is built upon the denigration of our fathers, our sons, and our lovers. We are continuing the time-honored tradition of dualistic thinking, a quality that we dislike profoundly in men.

The Inner Patriarch thrives on duality. He sees men and women as basically different, with men superior in every way. He separates the world into good and bad. *His* way is good, and everyone else's is bad. Men are inherently decent and good, and women are inherently untrustworthy and, possibly, even evil. He sees men as the creators and the upholders of the law, and women as the destroyers of law, order, and structure. If we fight the Inner Patriarch and make him the bad one, we are merely following his lead. We must strike out along a new path of our own.

*This path moves us beyond duality into unity, a unity that includes opposites at all times. Whenever we live in duality, there will be an "us" and a "them." In this case, it is women and men, or Matriarchs and Patriarchs. When we move beyond the opposites, we move to a "we," a broader definition of humankind. This section of the book traces this new path.*

The first steps along the path will take us to the recognition that the Inner Patriarch is not all bad. The chapter on "The Positive Aspects of the Inner Patriarch" shows us his contributions and his positive motivations. We see how we, as women, might learn something from his concerns about us and benefit from the gifts that he carries. Most important, however, in looking at his positive aspects, we move from an adversarial role to a cooperative one. We begin to move beyond duality to a consideration of how to live life standing between opposites; in this case, standing with one arm around the Inner Patriarch and the other around the Inner Matriarch. They are no longer authority figures whose orders must be followed, but have become allies and consultants.

The next step along the path takes us to the consideration of opposites. It is clear that the Inner Patriarch and the Inner Matriarch hold opposing views of the world, but there are other selves in women that are complementary to the Inner Patriarch. In the chapter called "Balancing the Power of the Inner Patriarch," these will be considered. The more clearly we can formulate these opposites, the easier it will be for us to balance the power of the Inner Patriarch and move beyond the dualistic universe in which he lives.

As we move beyond this duality, we enter an entirely new realm, the realm of the "Aware Ego." In the chapter entitled "Beyond Duality: The Realm of the Aware Ego," I will talk about this Aware Ego and its major role in turning the Inner Patriarch from an enemy into an ally.

Last, we, as humans, need entirely new skills in order to travel in this new realm. These skills are discussed in the chapter "Taking Command of Your Kingdom: Managing Your Energy Field." They are not gender specific, and they do not depend upon any particular physical or mental capabilities. Neither men nor women will naturally excel in these skills. Traditional education ignores them. This, too, is an area that Hal (my husband) and I have worked on collaboratively, and much of the information in these chapters comes directly from Hal's creativity.

Now, with these points in mind, let us begin to move along this new path.

# THE POSITIVE ASPECTS
# OF THE INNER PATRIARCH

*A woman of valor, who can find? For her price
is far above rubies. The heart of her husband
doth safely trust in her, and he hath no lack of
gain. She doeth him good and not evil all the
days of her life. She giveth food to her household, and a portion to her maidens. She stretcheth
out her hand to the poor; yea, she reacheth forth
her hands to the needy. Strength and dignity are
her clothing; and she laugheth at the time to
come. She openeth her mouth with wisdom, and
the law o' kindness is on her tongue. She
looketh well to the ways of her household and
eateth not the bread of idleness. Her children rise
up and call her blessed; her husband also and he
praiseth her: "Many daughters have done
valiantly, but thou excellest them all." Grace is
deceitful, and beauty is vain; but a woman that
revereth the Lord, she shall be praised. Give her
the fruit of her hands; and let her works praise
her at the gates.*

— Proverbs: Chapter 31:10-31

In most of our considerations of the Inner Patriarch, we have seen how he undermines women. His sense of their natural inferiority to men and his hopelessness about their chances for success in the world often discourage women from taking the steps they need in order to realize their full potential.

However, there are many ways in which the outer patriarchy has worked to support and protect women. As we get in touch with these protective and supportive aspects of our Inner Patriarch, we become able to maintain and, when necessary, defend our own boundaries.

Also, it's interesting to note that it is only in the countries of the first world where the patriarchy (of which we speak) has been strong, that the women have had the support and safety in which to explore these issues in the first place. *Our ability to question the patriarchal values is, at least in part, due to the protection afforded by those values themselves.*

### The Inner Patriarch as Rulemaker

This protection has been offered by the very rules and values that we are now re-examining. The Inner Patriarch, and the outer patriarchy as well, see themselves as the rulemakers of our particular civilization. In many areas of life, they have brought order out of chaos. They have made sure that this order is maintained and that the rules are followed. These rules have created the structure in which we live.

We should understand here that rules are not merely a way to wield power and to control others. Rules can create order, predictability, and safety. As we think about the rulemaking aspects of the Inner Patriarch, it's important to remember that rules define an agreement involving large numbers of people. We need, for example, to have all automobile drivers to agree to follow the rules that we drive on the same side of the road and stop at the red traffic lights. Similarly, constitutional government is a way of defining and defending what hopefully is a universally felt set of values, expressed in the form of rules.

*As the upholders of the traditional rules of the culture, our Inner Patriarchs have order, safety, security, predictability, and control as their goals.* If their rules are upheld, society should function as it always has, and we will all know our proper places. Our Inner Patriarchs become extremely anxious if anyone questions their rules. They are afraid of what might happen, and they truly fear that the world will fall into chaos if the rules are not followed. They do not trust people who are not following externally imposed rules; they know that people are capable of evil.

## A Woman Is Entitled to Support and Protection

*In his positive aspect, the Inner Patriarch honors the woman's traditional role in life and considers that she is entitled to admiration, support, and protection while she fulfills her obligations.* He does not require her to go out into the world and compete with men. Instead, he feels more comfortable when she is at home and properly cared for. He is very concerned about her safety in a man's world. He knows about her physical and emotional fragility and the dangers and difficulties of life. He wants to be sure that she does not have to face life alone because he fears that she is incapable of doing this effectively.

Therefore, he reasons, the best solution is to find a husband. As a matter of fact, it is very interesting to listen to the Inner Patriarch talk about a woman's choice of partner for relationship. Basically, the Inner Patriarch wants us as woman to have strong men to protect us in the world. He has little patience with men who lack male power. He is not at all interested in men's feelings, their ability to process, or in their sensitivities. He wants to know that they will be able to take care of us. We may feel his desires in this area as an almost instinctual pull towards a strong man even

127

though it might be at the expense of having men in our lives who are in touch with their feelings.

Our Inner Patriarchs cannot rest until there is a strong outer male in our lives, preferably one who can assume proper patriarchal power, to take over their duties and worries. *One of the difficulties these days is that women have a tendency to look for qualities in men that are not traditionally male, and this makes their Inner Patriarchs very uncomfortable. This disparity between the desires of the woman and those of her Inner Patriarch can be extremely confusing to men, who find that they are being asked to be sensitive and understanding, but when they truly achieve this, they are rejected. They no longer know what it is that women want.* I talked about this topic briefly in the chapter on "The Inner Patriarch and Relationship." Now let us look at how it works in Alexandra's life.

Alexandra was a professional woman and quite definitive about her desires in terms of relationship. She had done her own psychological work and was quite clear that she wanted a man who would be different from her father. She wanted a man who would be in touch with his feelings and responsive to hers. She wanted a partner, an equal in life. When she found Greg, it seemed as though it was the perfect match. Greg was sensitive and respectful. They could talk for hours, sharing their feelings and their ideas. They saw eye to eye on just about everything. Greg could even cry with her.

But something seemed to be bothering Alexandra. She was very confused. Although Greg seemed to be everything she wanted in a man, she found herself becoming critical of precisely those qualities that she wanted in him. When we talked to her Inner Patriarch, we discovered the problem. This is what he had to say about Greg's feelings and his ability to cry:

*Sidra:* What do you say when her partner is upset?

*Inner Patriarch:* I ask her what she's done wrong and let her know that she had better do something quickly to fix it. For instance, when he cries, I tell her that she must have done something wrong.

*Sidra:* How do you feel about his crying?

*Inner Patriarch:* I don't like it. It makes me uncomfortable. When her father complained, he never cried. He was stoic and serious and only complained about what was wrong at work. You'd never see him cry. That was for her mother.

First of all, we must remember that the Inner Patriarch's rules are the rules! If a man is unhappy, it is the woman's fault and she should fix it immediately. Sharing feelings with a girlfriend, empathizing with her sadness and allowing her to feel it is fine, but your man is a different story. You cannot just sit there and allow him to be sad; you must fix him. A sad man is the sign of an inadequate woman. When your man is sad, you have failed him somehow or somewhere.

Secondly, Alexandra's Inner Patriarch did not respect Greg at all. He wanted Alexandra to have a real man, one who knew how to wield his power, one who was not unduly influenced by his feelings and who could be tough when necessary. Her Inner Patriarch saw Greg as inadequate to the task ahead, the task of protecting Alexandra. Needless to say, this double message communicated itself to Greg and made him quite uncomfortable.

Once Alexandra saw the source of her ambivalence, she was able to work with her Inner Patriarch and deal with his discomfort directly. Together, she and Greg were able to get in touch with the positive intentions that their Inner Patriarchs shared and work mutually to protect and care for one another and their relationship. *The Inner Patriarch is like a father who is concerned about the welfare of his daughter. He cannot rest until she is safe.* When he searches for a "real man," someone he believes will be able to care for her properly, he is trying to protect her and to secure her future to the best of his ability. The moment he sees that the woman is truly safe and secure, whether on her own or in a relationship, the Inner Patriarch can relax. This part of his job is done. From then on, he is more like a consultant than a father, and provides a constant source of positive counsel and support.

### Sexual Protection

*The Inner Patriarch takes responsibility for protecting women from their own, and others', sexuality.* Underneath it all, he is terrified of sexuality, particularly women's sexuality. He fears that left to their own devices, women would be unrestrainedly promiscuous and totally out of control. He also fears the effect that women's undisciplined sexuality, or even their sensuality, might have upon men. He is concerned that women could drive men beyond their own ability to control themselves.

As a young girl's sensuality begins to emerge, her Inner Patriarch begins to exert his control. He is alert to the dangers in her own home. He fears her natural sensuality. He is cautious about allowing her to express herself in a flirtatious fashion and is critical or even abusive in his comments about her sexuality. He lets her know that her sensuality is dangerous and that it will bring her nothing but grief if it is expressed fully. He may even tell her that her sensuality is truly disgusting and should be denied.

As the Inner Patriarch gains power in her early years, usually at about the age of five or six, there are three types of family situations that strengthen his concerns about the young girl's sensuality or sexuality: (1) In households where the father is a substance abuser and has impaired impulse control, it is often the daughter's Inner Patriarch who protects her from the possibility of sexual molestation. (2) In households where the relationship between the husband and wife is not fulfilling and the father has transferred his primary feelings of love and closeness to his daughter, the daughter's Inner Patriarch often senses a possible danger and begins to rein in her own sensuality early to protect this loving closeness and to avert possible sexual involvement. (3) The third kind of household is one in which there are very strict moral injunctions about sexuality, and it is the daughter's Inner Patriarch who picks up these injunctions and enforces them so that she can remain acceptable to her family.

Unfortunately, this protection frequently involves the negation of the girl's sexuality. Jolie, for instance, was extremely uncomfortable about her sexuality when she first came to work with us. She was overweight and dressed in a most unflattering fashion. She did everything she could to deaden any possibility of sexual provocation. When I talked to her Inner Patriarch about this, he agreed that it was important to play down Jolie's sexuality. He spoke at great length about how distasteful he found women's sexuality, and that other males agreed with him.

When we talked about his reasons for being so critical and controlling, Jolie's Inner Patriarch was quick to point out that her father was a drinking man who loved her a bit too much and, at the same time, was not very fond of his wife. Jolie's Inner Patriarch felt that it was very important to squelch her sexuality. If not, he was quite sure that Jolie's sexuality would have been too great a temptation for her father and that he would have crossed the incest boundary and become sexually involved with her. In this way, both Jolie and her father were protected by her Inner Patriarch.

Lottie's Inner Patriarch was similarly concerned about her sexuality. He needed to do something about it to protect her from her father. As he put it, he "had to have the colors eaten away from the very colorful little girl that Lottie used to be, because this little girl had been far too colorful, so colorful in fact that her father had been abusing her." Once these colors were eaten away, Lottie was safe from her father. She associated only with little boys, not girls, and she played and acted like a boy. She was colorful only

131

when alone. Her Inner Patriarch, in order to protect her, had forced her to disown her Aphrodite nature. He made her so ashamed of her sexuality that the worst thing anyone could say to her was that she was beautiful or sexy. This would make her ashamed and shy, and she would cry. Although his method may seem harsh to some, Lottie's Inner Patriarch did what he could to protect her from a very damaging situation.

*This is a good time to give the Inner Patriarchs the credit they deserve for upholding the incest taboo in this society!* It is the man's Patriarch that is primarily responsible for controlling the father's sexual behavior when he is faced with a daughter who blossoms into a woman while living in his home, a woman whom he has loved since birth.

### Relationship as Sacred

*When we think nostalgically of the "good old days" when most marriages lasted a lifetime, the family unit was sacred, and our country was not distressed by a divorce rate of approximately 50 percent, we might give the Inner Patriarch a word of thanks. The Inner Patriarch is a relentless supporter and protector of relationship. He actually knows a great deal about the ingredients of a good relationship, even though he tends to apportion these ingredients along gender lines.* In his support of relationship, the Inner Patriarch treats it as the highest calling of a woman. He sees the marriage relationship as truly holy and will have the woman do anything in her power to preserve it. Alive and well within us, he is a staunch defender of the family unit and does not see any possible excuse for breaking it up.

The Inner Patriarch is a traditionalist in his views of how relationships would be protected, however. For him, feminine behavior in a relationship involves receptivity, nonassertiveness, feeling, intuition, nurturing, weakness, and dependence. In return, a woman has the right to be protected and cared for. When asked about his rules for a women's behavior with a man, Nora's Inner Patriarch put it this way:

> *Inner Patriarch:* I wish she were more like her mother. Her mother knew how to be with a man. Her mother would always be there and interested. Her father would come home at night and sit in his comfortable chair in the kitchen and tell her about how hard his day was. Then her mother would sympathize with him. It was really good. But she isn't like her mother; she doesn't know how to nurture a man. When she gives, it's cold and unrelated. She doesn't know how to be a woman. Her mother knew how. Her mother stayed married to the same man. Nora is so selfish that every man is going to leave her. She left her husband and has hurt her children irreparably, and I'll never forgive her for this.

> *Sidra:* Are the children having problems?

> *Inner Patriarch:* Not that you can see, but they're there underneath, and they'll never get over them, and it's all her fault.

While on the surface, Nora's Inner Patriarch is being very hard on her and really putting her down, we should not lose sight of his positive intentions and the useful content in his message. He wants her to take care of her husband so that her husband will want to take care of her. The Inner Patriarch is one of the voices in Nora that wants her to be more nurturing, more caring, and more supportive. Certainly, these self-sacrificing urges in women have gotten out of control in the past! Nevertheless, within a family system, these are worthwhile qualities that help to ensure that family members get the emotional warmth and support they need.

We might note that the Inner Patriarch expects a great deal of women, but he expects a great deal of men as well. In contrast to what he wants from a woman, the Inner Patriarch wants men to carry strength, aggression, assertiveness, economic responsibility, responsibility for the safety and stability of others, and objectivity and the ability to ignore feelings. If the man does this, the Inner Patriarch reasons that the relationship and the family will be adequately protected.

## When Men and Women Need Each Other

Interestingly enough, this definitive set of rules of behavior and the clearly differentiated gender roles for men and women create a situation in which males and females will be attracted to one another. They complement one another and are mutually dependent. If everyone follows these rules, both men and women find that they need each other for completion. Neither can manage well alone.

In the beginning of this book, we spoke about primary and disowned selves in relationship. Primary selves are those that develop to protect us in the world. They are the building blocks of our personality. They make us who we are. Conversely, the disowned selves are the opposite selves, the selves that we reject. When we live life out of our primary selves, we lose our access to the gifts carried by our disowned selves.

As if searching for some way to regain something mysterious that we have lost, we are irresistibly attracted to people who carry these disowned selves for us. We love them, we overvalue them, and we judge them. In our own process of growth, we need to incorporate some aspect of our disowned selves to become whole. I am not suggesting that we let our disowned selves take over our lives. Heavens no! This gives us as little choice as we had originally when we were identified with our primary selves. No, we do not need to become our disowned selves; for example, women do not need to overthrow the Inner Patriarch and become men, but we do need to have more balance and some choices. I will speak later about how we can do so, and how our actions also can free the men in our lives.

Now we'll go back to the way in which the Inner Patriarch has made relationships between men and women so very important. *Since his emphasis is upon clearly differentiated roles, this provides an immediate set of disowned selves that would attract men and women to one another and that would automatically require men and women to come together to complete themselves.* As women, we find our own disowned male in the men in our lives. Conversely, the man finds his disowned female in the women in his life. The pull towards the disowned self often feels absolutely irresistible. This is the strong feeling of "my other half" that was so prevalent and admired in the past.

## Men Need Their Patriarchs

As the women's movement has gained momentum and power, more and more men have been told that the patriarchy and male values are destructive. Many men, fearful of becoming bullies, have embraced a more traditionally feminine primary self system, have listened to their Inner Matriarchs, and have disowned their own Patriarchs. This can be a serious problem because *both men and women need the strengths that the Patriarch carries.* Moreover, the woman who has disowned her own Inner Patriarch will not be able to find it in the man who has disowned his.

The following is an excerpt from a Voice Dialogue session with Bert, who actually *had* disowned his Patriarch. Bert had lived with a spiritual group that disapproved of the outer patriarchy and systematically did away with his Patriarch and its demands. Without the strength and guidance of this Patriarch which, in the past, had shown him how to live like a man, Bert had become anxious, unsure of himself, and unfocused.

*Sidra:* Tell me about your rules for how Bert should behave in relationship.

*Bert's Patriarch* (at the moment, a disowned self): He should be a man! I'm ashamed of him, of the way he cries so easily. He has already used up all the tears that he should have in any one relationship in the first few months of this one. It embarrasses me if he cries. I have changed. I do believe that men can have feelings, but they should not be led around by them. He is too soft; he feels too much. He is still moaning about the loss of his ashram and his last relationship. This woman is going to leave him if he doesn't stop it. He's always feeling and feeling and processing and processing.

*Sidra:* If he were a woman, would it be okay if he were still mourning this loss?

*Patriarch:* Yes, you expect women to mourn longer and to feel more, but he should be over it by now. He has no strength. A man should have strength.

*Sidra:* You look like *you* have strength.

*Patriarch:* I certainly do. A real man should have a steel bar down his back so that he can take whatever life gives him. He should stay strong no matter what happens. This guy's a wimp! Always feeling and complaining.

*Sidra:* What about how he does at work? He's got a lot to get done before he leaves on vacation. What would you have him do differently?

*Patriarch:* I'd have him set priorities and stick to them. I'd have him concentrate. He's too busy feeling and going with the flow. I believe in discipline [this said with real power and objectivity]. I'd have him look over everything and see what will blow up if he leaves it for five weeks.

I'd have him take care of those things. If he can't finish them, I'd have him take them with him so that they don't blow up while he's gone. He can finish things up on vacation. As for the rest, I'd tell him to leave it. He thinks that he has to get everything done. That's just not true. He's too scared to leave anything. As I said, he's gotten too emotional.

For instance, now he's nervous and he wants to back up all his hard disks. He hasn't done this in the past six years, and he wants to do it now that he's getting ready to leave on vacation. It's terrible timing. As far as I am concerned, all the important things have been backed up in the past couple of days. Now he should get these backups out of the house and put them in a safe place. He doesn't have to bother about anything else.

This is just an excerpt from a longer session in which Bert's Patriarch gave a number of additional suggestions for life, for work, and for better organization. As a result of this session, Bert realized that he had indeed thrown out the baby with the bath water. He needed the focus and the objectivity of his Patriarch.

Much to his own relief and, I might add, the relief of his wife, Bert reclaimed his Patriarch. This helped him to get organized, calm his anxieties, and to live life with greater ease and authority. Bert did not become his Patriarch; he just reclaimed him and used him as a consultant whose suggestions could be followed or rejected. "Employing" the Inner Patriarch as a consultant in our lives allows us to listen to his opinions and weigh the pros and cons of his advice without blindly complying or, on the other hand, feeling anxious or inadequate because we are rejecting him or fighting with him.

## Women Need Their Inner Patriarchs, Too

One of the interesting aspects of exploring our inner worlds is the element of surprise. You never really know what you're going to discover. *One of the more surprising discoveries I made was that the Inner Patriarch is quite often right when he talks about men. After all, he is one. Just as he keeps telling us, we women do need our Inner Patriarchs to help us with the care and nurturing of our relationships.*

The first time I noticed this was when I was discussing relationship with Corinne, a woman who had not experienced much success in her relationships with men. Nothing ever seemed to work out for her. She had great male friends, but no lovers. As we talked about this, I discovered that Corinne's mother had very carefully avoided teaching her daughter any of the lessons that her own mother had taught her about men and relationships.

Corinne' mother wanted her to be free and equal in all of her male/female relationships. The women in their family had traditionally been the victims of domineering males and Corinne's mother did not want this tradition continued. She had done her own work in learning about this victimization, both historically and personally, and she was very careful not to teach Corinne any of the "old patriarchal" values. In fact, her lifestyle prevented Corinne from even learning about these values.

This had a surprising effect. Corinne did not know how to be with a man. She didn't have a clue about being feminine. She was identified with her independent and equal woman and had disowned the Inner Patriarch completely. It was not even an issue in her life. Corinne actually suffered a great deal as a result. She could see that other women apparently had the ability to attract men and maintain relationships, but she did not know what it was they were doing.

I could see that Corinne was lacking the basic information that the Inner Patriarch, as a male advisor, supplies. This does not mean that if she were to have the information, she would have to listen to all of it or that she had to become a victim. *But lacking this basic information, she could not make an informed choice about how to behave! Besides, as the old saying goes, it always helps to know the rules before you decide to break them* .

Since my initial meeting with Corinne, I have met a number of other women who did not have any access to their Inner Patriarchs. They all had similar difficulties in their relationships with men.

### Abuse of Power

Up until now, I have talked about the ways in which the Inner Patriarch has tried to support us within our individual lives. Now I would like to look outward, to a somewhat broader picture. One of the Inner Patriarch's concerns is the abuse of power. Much of our patriarchal legal system involves apportioning power fairly among people. The proper balance of power is usually a major consideration.

Since the Inner Patriarch is sensitive to this issue, he will curb a woman (or even a man for that matter) if at any time he feels that she is taking unfair advantage of her position. Although, as we saw in the chapter on the Inner Patriarch and Power, his containment of women's power has been excessive, there are times when his warnings are appropriate. Again, let us not throw out the baby with the bath water.

We women have needed to take our power over the last 30 years without worrying about whether or not we were going too far. We had come from a system in which we were basically disrespected, totally dominated, and where we essentially had no rights, power, or control over our lives. We needed to be warriors in order to take this power, very often from people who were less than willing to relinquish it. A total change in consciousness was necessary. This was no time to think about fairness, moderation, or balance. We owe deep respect and gratitude to the women who led this movement and brought us this enormous distance. Sensitivity to remaining inequities, or to the re-emergence of old inequities is still imperative.

However, we have come far enough to move towards a more balanced point of view. In the past we have had to be constantly on guard and reactive. Now we can begin to think about balance and fairness. We can afford to look at the opposite points of view as well as our own. If we always need to be right and powerful, we run the risk of being unfair and unbalanced. We might even unnecessarily draw towards ourselves the envy and anger of others. *In its positive aspects, our Inner Patriarch's rules about fairness and sensitivity to the abuse of power can protect us as women from the envy and the power of others.*

### The Good of the Group Is More Important Than the Well-being of Any Individual Member

The Inner Patriarch is one of the inner voices that attends to the best interests of the group and puts these before the interests of the individual. Thus, the group is protected, and its survival is ensured. He is afraid that if women were left to their own devices, they would ignore the rules of civilization and would not discipline themselves properly.

With his ability to be impersonal about life, the Inner Patriarch can calculate the possible dangers of reacting emotionally to a situation. For instance, if someone is in danger, but rescuing this single person would imperil the rest of the group, he could make the decision to abandon the person who needs help. Without his help and his support in standing firm, a woman is likely to put aside the welfare of the group if someone she loves is threatened.

*The Inner Patriarch can also make difficult decisions about cutting back. Whether this is in cutting back the growth in a garden, curbing inappropriate behavior in children, or trimming a budget, the Inner Patriarch can help us make these decisions. He has an objectivity that cannot be swayed by emotions.* Of course, his objectivity needs to be balanced by emotional considerations, but if we do not have his invaluable input available, we run the risk of a serious imbalance in all of our decision making.

We have looked at some of the positive contributions of the Inner Patriarch, and you might consider which of these you would want to preserve. Now let us move on to consider the ways in which his negative impact upon us, as women, can be balanced.

# BALANCING THE POWER OF THE INNER PATRIARCH

*The more clearly we can formulate the oppo-
sites, the easier it will be for us to balance the
power of the Inner Patriarch and move beyond
the dualistic universe in which he lives.*

There are a number of selves other than the Matriarch that balance the Inner Patriarch. Each has something to contribute to women, and each is quite different in the role that it plays. In our move toward empowerment as women, we must learn to stand between opposites, between the power of the selves in us that carries the traditionally masculine qualities and values (like the Inner Patriarch) and those that carry the traditionally feminine ones. *This means that we have to claim the gifts of our Inner Patriarchs and use these gifts consciously while, at the same time, we keep the gifts that have been traditionally feminine and treat these with the respect and honor that they deserve.*

The first of these selves are what I think of as the traditionally feminine selves. They complement the Inner Patriarch and support him. They admire his traditionally masculine qualities, and when they come together with a male who carries these qualities, they are very happy and feel quite complete. This type of self was embodied in Melanie, the gentlewoman who contrasts with Scarlett O'Hara, the powerful and independent heroine of *Gone With the Wind.* She carried all the traditional graces of the female

143

and, in her marriage, she came together with the traditional man, Ashley, in such a way that they fit perfectly, each carrying one-half of the necessary skills for living life. They completed one another.

The second set of selves comprise the less domesticated selves, what we might think of as natural or feral women. The gypsies, the wanderers, the wild wolves and jaguars, and the bag ladies, too, all belong here. It is this group of selves that Clarissa Pinkola-Estes showed us in her book, *Women Who Run With Wolves*. There is another group as well. These are the pre-adolescent boys and girls, the selves that have not yet been tamed or civilized. All these selves emphasize freedom from the rules that govern acceptable female behavior, particularly the rules about marriage and home life. These selves have a need to live an independent life and to create what needs to be created. They follow their instincts and their passions.

The third set of selves are the power selves. The Matriarch in the previous chapter is one of these power selves. The remainder of the power selves are *not* the opposite of the Inner Patriarch, rather they are selves that carry his attributes and skills. Many of the militant feminists use these power selves to the exclusion of the traditionally feminine ones. These selves neutralize the negative power of the Inner Patriarch and enable women to operate with great authority in the world of men. Now let us consider all of these selves in more detail.

### The Traditionally Feminine Selves

*The traditionally feminine selves are the complements of the Inner Patriarch. They love his power and are glad to have him carry the authority as long as he also carries the responsibility. They enjoy caring for the hearth and the home. They love the man to be strong in the world and they, in turn, are delighted to take care of him and bring the gentleness and peace to life. They do not feel superior to the man because of this, like the Matriarch does. They do not mock him when he is not*

144

around. They feel that this is the way things should be in this world, and they are proud to be playing the feminine role. There was much emphasis upon developing these selves in the 1950s, and they are still pervasive in the more fundamentalist religions.

These selves present a major paradox. On the one hand, they carry traditional feminine attributes and values, and they are greatly encouraged by the Inner Patriarch from the shadows in which he operates. On the other hand, however, as much as the Inner Patriarch supports these selves as the primary ones for women, he does not respect them. How does this work?

Let us take Melanie from *Gone With the Wind* as an example of a woman with these traditionally feminine primary selves. She is an ideal Consort/Wife to her husband, and a loving, Nurturing Mother to everyone she knows. Her Aphrodite Self is devoted to the relationship with her husband. She is loving, giving, sensitive, delicate, understanding, self-sacrificing, trusting, supportive of those she loves, and totally dependent upon others to protect her in the world outside her home. Her Inner Patriarch encourages all this; he is happy with Melanie as a truly feminine woman who has fulfilled her mission in life. Her primary selves are the proper ones; she is a good woman and is in relationship with a man who adores her.

However, her Inner Patriarch, the Shadow King, carries all her disowned power. He carries the strengths she lacks. He is disowned, which means that he lives in her unconscious. She does not know that he is there, operating in the shadows, dictating the basic rules for her existence and encouraging her dependence and her innocence. Even though she is following his dictates, Melanie's Inner Patriarch does not value her as a complete, independent human being. He knows that although she has her special feminine strengths, she cannot survive in the world. She must be cared for. The Inner Patriarch does not respect people who cannot care for themselves.

Now let us look at these primary selves in more detail. The first of them is a self that I think of as the Consort or Wife of the patriarch; perhaps she is what the Matriarch was like before she became disillusioned, bitter, and angry. This Consort/Wife emphasizes the importance of the relationship and is willing to sacrifice much for her relationships. She is capable of being dependent, of taking from another. Her ideal is a relationship between equals, each of whom contributes something priceless. In her ability to be dependent and in her wish for equality in relationship, she is the opposite of the Inner Patriarch. He despises dependence and is basically more interested in domination than in equality.

This Consort/Wife almost has a sacred sound when she speaks. Her voice is soft, gentle, and musical. Again, this contrasts sharply with the Inner Patriarch, whose voice is strong, powerful, and commanding. *The Consort/Wife speaks of the coming together of opposites, of moving beyond duality to oneness. This is not an abstract principle for her. She sees it in very personal terms, in the coming together of the male and the female.* As Cornelia's Consort/Wife says in a hushed, reverent voice:

> Once upon a time, a long time ago, the Patriarch and I were married. We were very happy together. But then something happened, and we were separated. We were split off into two different parts and were sent into different parts of the world, and we began to hate one another. I became an angry Matriarch, but I have missed him terribly. I want to be back with him again. Together we are whole; separate we are not happy.
>
> I love it when he (the Patriarch) takes care of me. I also love it when he takes care of financial matters. I hate to think about them. In this way I do not have to worry about the world, and I can bring him what he needs. I can be his other half. I can teach him to be feeling and gentle, and when he is, I am so very happy! Then, someday when I am together with the Patriarch once again, we

will go back, back beyond time to the place where we
both were one. That is the way it should be.

The Nurturing Mother is the second of the traditional feminine
selves that complements the Inner Patriarch beautifully. She plays
"mother" to his "father." She does not struggle for equal power; in
fact, she is not interested in power at all. She has no desire to compete in the same arena as the man. She nurtures and cares for people, while the man in her life protects them. She is happy to
sacrifice herself for the well-being of others. Actually, she would
not think in terms of sacrifice. Her greatest joy is to nurture those
she loves.

The Nurturing Mother has an almost holy quality about her. She
is supported by the Inner Patriarch, but she is not truly valued by
him. She does not provide anyone with "billable hours," that is,
hours of work for which one can charge a fee. She does not produce a tangible product that can be sold. In a patriarchal system,
her gifts may be extolled, but her efforts have no worth in the marketplace. A woman who is identified with this Nurturing Mother
as a primary self, someone who lives only as a mother or caregiver
to others, is not able to take care of herself in the world. Her Inner
Patriarch does not respect her and does not consider her safe because she is not able to see to it that her own needs (be they physical, financial, or emotional) are properly met. These days he will
call her co-dependent, which she is. However, in denigrating her
contributions to our quality of life—both for ourselves and for
those around us—we lose much.

*When Nola's Nurturing Mother spoke, she had overtones of the Vir-
gin Mary. She was so filled with understanding, love, compassion, and
a quiet sort of joy, that she looked radiant. I thought of Quan Yin, the
Chinese goddess of compassion and mercy. Everyone who came to her
would feel blessed by the warmth of this being. This Nurturing Mother
had great strength even though it was basically very gentle.* She spoke
of her recent Christmas celebration as follows:

I had such a wonderful time. The children were all home for the holidays. Our closest friends came to stay with us. I was so happy. I decorated the house and the tree. I thought carefully and I bought special presents for everyone and wrapped them. I felt so good doing that. I could just picture each person's joy at what I was giving.

Then I cooked and I cooked. I baked delicious things, cookies and cakes. I made some food before and I froze it. Then, after everybody came, I cooked other food. The house smelled so good. And I planned it so carefully that I had plenty of time with everyone. It's true that I didn't get much sleep, but I think that it was the happiest vacation of my entire life.

Needless to say, this Nurturing Mother makes the Inner Patriarch very happy, and when he is happy and gives his approval, a woman can feel very good. She "knows" that she is doing the right thing because she is getting rewarded. She can relax. However, *unlike the Inner Patriarch, the Nurturing Mother does not feel that power is the most important aspect of life; she believes that love and caring for others is even more important. Thus, when her values are also incorporated into one's world view, and the Inner Patriarch no longer dominates the value system, balance is introduced into a woman's psyche.* There are other ways in which the Nurturing Mother and the Inner Patriarch can come together creatively, as you will see in the following story.

I have heard it said that the most beautiful songs on earth are those that are heard only by children. They are the songs that the mothers, these nurturing mothers, sing. They are songs that come directly from a loving heart and from the depths of the soul that recognizes and cherishes another.

As the Nurturing Mother self or archetype becomes more valued, the men of the world can begin to gain access to her. As men are allowed into the nursery, as they are welcomed into the traditionally feminine field of child care and childrearing, they, too, can experience the beauty and depth of this archetypal experience.

A well known cellist, Julian Lloyd Webber, told movingly of his personal experience with this archetypally feminine self (although he did not speak of it in these terms). He spoke of practicing his cello with his infant daughter sleeping in a cradle next to him. As he played, he watched her sleep, and as he looked at her, something happened to him. We could say that this archetypal Nurturing Mother awakened within him. Julian had never written any music before, but a hauntingly beautiful song, a song of the soul, arose within him. He stopped his playing and wrote it down. He was so entranced by this cradle music or lullaby, that he began to research other songs of this type. He, or this Nurturing Mother, found that there was something quite special about them. He collected the very best and made a CD of them. This is truly an act that combines the gifts of the Inner Patriarch (research, discipline, knowledge, producing a saleable product) with the gifts of loving, unself-conscious creativity carried by the Nurturing Mother.

This picture of Julian Lloyd Webber playing the cello and just being quiet with his infant daughter naturally leads to a description of the third of the traditionally feminine selves. This is a self that Hal and I call the "Being" self, in contrast to the "Doing" selves so very much valued by the Inner Patriarch. Like the Nurturing Mother, this Being self does not produce much that we could consider practical or useful. Instead, it knows how to relax, to be in the moment, and to allow thoughts, feelings, and impressions to bubble up from our very depths.

*This "Being" self has been described by some as the "receptive feminine." It contrasts sharply with the traditionally masculine values of doing, accomplishing, and producing that are so important to the Inner Patriarchs of the world. When it is operating, we can connect deeply and quietly with others. Time stops, and the moment seems to become expanded and magical. We have no need to impress others with our wit, our wisdom, or our accomplishments. Conversely, we are not particularly*

149

*impressed with theirs. Instead, we are just two human beings together enjoying one another.*

In a patriarchal society such as ours, this Being self is disowned in favor of achievement, and I feel that there is a great need for all of us, both men and women, to reclaim this lost part of our heritage. As I look around me, I see that over the last several decades, life has speeded up considerably and there is less and less space for just being. People are constantly busy, and our Inner Patriarchs are fearful that if we stop for even a moment, everyone else will move out ahead of us and we will lose our place in the world.

Our Inner Patriarch echoes the values of this patriarchal world in which we live. He admires its achievements which have, indeed, been absolutely stunning! This is not the place to laud these achievements in detail, but they are staggering, and the quality of our lives has been remarkably improved. In addition, we can accomplish tasks that would have taken weeks or months or even years in very little time and with a minimum of effort.

On the other hand, however, the average American's work week has expanded, and the concept of time off or quiet weekends has all but disappeared. Years ago, stores were closed on the weekends and in the evenings. There were things that you just could not do at night or on a Sunday, so it was easier to slow down or just to "be" rather than "do." Now we can shop, work, learn, or communicate with others 24 hours a day, 7 days a week. There are no external limitations. Our access to information and communication is instantaneous, with computers, faxes, e-mail, cellular phones, and beepers.

There is no reason not to be productive. That is, our Inner Patriarchs (and the outer ones, too) can see no reason for us to stop producing. Again, it is the traditionally feminine selves, like the Wife/Consort, the Nurturing Mother, the Being self—and the Inner Matriarch as well—who see life differently. They carry the opposite values that can help us balance what is essentially a one-sided view of life.

Let us move on now to the last of these traditionally feminine selves, the Aphrodite self. She, too, complements the Inner Patriarch. She is the one who values attraction, sensuality, feminine charms, and love as the last of the traditional feminine selves. Instead of devaluing sensuality and distrusting romantic attractions, she exalts these. She is committed to love and beauty. When a woman has access to this self, she is attractive to men and has a certain power all her own.

*If a woman truly knows her Aphrodite nature, she has had her birthright returned to her. She will be able to enjoy herself as a woman. She will feel good about her body and enjoy the sensual pleasures of life. She will attract others to her and enjoy this attraction. She will not be apologetic.* But, if she has a strong Inner Patriarch, she will be required to temper this self and to use it primarily in the service of a marital relationship.

When a woman has any of these traditionally feminine selves as a dominant part of her personality, her Inner Patriarch is usually very, very strong and very unconscious. He will support the men in her relationships and keep her (the woman) in a more submissive position. He protects the man, and the man's needs, in the relationship.

However, *when a woman has access not only to these traditionally feminine selves, but to the power and objectivity of her Inner Patriarch as well, she stands between opposites. She has the power of the Inner Patriarch available to her from within. She can use this power consciously, and she does not need to rely upon the outer males to supply this power in her life. Instead, her relationships with men are on a more equal footing and, therefore, more rewarding.* She can balance these opposites of femininity and traditional masculine power as she sees fit and can move through life with choice. She moves beyond duality.

### The Natural Woman

*The Natural Woman is the self who carries the instincts that are our natural way of being in the world. She can experience our moods and reactions, our passions and our needs. She is not domesticated. She would not think of putting the needs of others before her own, or of trying to please them.* Many women see this self as an animal rather than a woman; usually as a member of the cat family, such as a lioness, a panther, or a jaguar. Recently, more women see the wolf as carrying this independent, untamed energy.

Surprisingly enough, this naturalness is sometimes carried within women not by a female self, but by a pre-adolescent boy self of nine or ten. These young boy selves are still free of societal restraints and requirements. One such self was described as a "snot-nosed little boy." This ten-year-old boy was totally shameless, fearless, and very colorful. He loved being the center of attention and wanted everyone to see and hear him. He could do anything without shyness or self-consciousness. It is the requirement of the Inner Patriarch that the young girl give up her color and intensity. This requirement makes a girl self-conscious and shy about all of her natural instincts and particularly self-conscious about her sexuality.

The Natural Woman is free from such rules. The Inner Patriarch fears her. He stands for rules and self-restraint. We, as women, can listen to her wishes and to his fears and move beyond the duality that these two competing world views create, combining them into a new inclusive whole that takes both their needs and concerns into consideration.

Carla, the woman whose Inner Patriarch spoke in Chapter Two, looked for a natural self of this type. She felt the need for an energy or a self that would provide a balance for her Inner Patriarch's traditional and somewhat restricted view of life. What she found was a gypsy who was clearly one of these natural women. This gypsy was free to do as she wished, free from the ordinary expectations of wife and mother.

This was accomplished through Voice Dialogue—that is, by directly addressing the selves. This was how we found out about Carla's Inner Patriarch and his beliefs in the first place. When he spoke the words I quoted in Chapter Two, he was sitting in his own chair, a chair that was reserved for him by Carla. She had moved over and sat in it so that he could establish his own space and his own individuality. After her Inner Patriarch finished talking, Carla stood up and returned to her own original chair, the seat of her Aware Ego. This is the part of her that can move beyond duality and embrace opposites. But before she can embrace the opposites, she has to know what self lives on the other side. Carla then moved to a chair opposite to the Inner Patriarch's and waited to see who would appear to carry the opposing energy. For her, this turned out to be a gypsy.

This Gypsy self felt very alive and vibrant. When she talked, Carla's body came alive. She did not want Carla to wear a bra. Instead, she liked the feeling of freedom and sensuality of going braless. She enjoyed wearing beautiful colors and long dangly earrings. She liked to be in the country, and wanted Carla to relax, to try new things in her therapy practice, to have fun, and to enjoy herself. The Gypsy said she was really worried about Carla, that she was too tense and discontent, that she would die like the babies who fail to thrive because they are not held.

This Gypsy self said that she is allowed out during vacations because the Inner Patriarch does not care about vacations. Vacations are not a part of real life. The Gypsy also pointed out that it was she who had originally gotten together with a Gypsy part of Carla's husband and had started their romance. (As you can gather from the earlier discussions of the Inner Patriarch's need to find a woman a husband, he is happy to use whatever selves are necessary to do so. Once they have served their purposes, they, like Carla's Gypsy, are safely tucked away where they will not do any damage.) Now that the Inner Patriarch had taken over Carla's life, the two Gypsies never seemed to get together at all.

Obviously, this Gypsy, with her natural zest for life, would bring Carla a great deal of excitement and enjoyment. She would go far in balancing the Inner Patriarch. However, it will be extremely important for Carla to move beyond the dualistic system and to include the needs of both selves as she moves through life. Only an Aware Ego can do this, and you will hear more about this Aware Ego in the next chapter.

As I have said, it is not only through Voice Dialogue that these balancing selves can be contacted. Maya, a friend of mine, told me of a beautiful and powerful experience in which her natural woman had emerged spontaneously. Maya is a woman with a strong Inner Patriarch who operates in the shadows, dictating rules that she must follow. He usually controls her behavior completely, keeping her fairly subdued and proper.

Quite recently, Maya was at a week-long residential workshop with a group of women. Each evening there was beautiful music, and the women danced. But the dancing was not exciting. The women were cautious and controlled. As Maya said:

> I know how I felt, and I suppose that the others felt pretty much the same as I did. Anyway, they looked as though they did. I felt very self-conscious. I was afraid of letting my energies get expansive and free. I was afraid of moving too much, that I would take up too much space. I was uncomfortable moving my body in any ways that might be considered provocative because there were gay women there who might think that I was flirting with them, and I did not want them to think I was encouraging them. It was not a very enjoyable experience.
>
> Then on the third night, something very interesting happened. One of the women took off her blouse and started to dance. Then another woman and another did

it. The group leader slithered out of all her clothes and began to dance naked. The rest of us dropped our clothes, and it seemed as though we dropped our inhibitions with them. We danced and we danced! We moved freely and magnificently. We were not afraid to bump up against one another. I have never seen women so fluid and so gorgeous. It was stunning!

There were old women and young women. The oldest was 75, and the youngest was 17. There were women with two breasts, women with one breast, and women with no breasts. There were women with scars, and women without them. There were straight women and gay women. Everyone was glowing and glorious! It was the most amazing and wonderful experience of pure freedom and naturalness I have ever had.

One of the most interesting things that I noticed about this evening was that it was pure sensuality and movement. There was nothing sexual or suggestive about it even though none of us had clothes on. There was a way in which being in our bodies in this way was totally comfortable, totally ordinary. There was no trying to be anything or to control anything; there was just being with the music and with ourselves. There was no awkwardness and no self-consciousness.

*The natural woman is aware of her body and comfortable with it. She is aware of her emotions, and she acts upon them easily. She can be ferocious when necessary.* Many women use a kind of totem animal to give themselves a feeling of this natural woman. See which one speaks to you. Would it be a jaguar slinking through the rain forest, ready to pounce? Would it be an eagle soaring high above, strong, all-seeing, and free of all worldly commitments? Maybe it would be a hawk riding the updrafts and feeling the joyous lift of the air currents. Or a dolphin playing in the waves, a moving, sensing part of all that surrounds it. Perhaps it would be a cat who always knows what feels good, how to take care of herself, and where to find the best place to sleep in the sun.

If you enjoy reading, there is no better place to go to find out about your own natural, instinctual, soulful, undomesticated woman than to Clarissa Pinkola-Estes' book, *Women Who Run with the Wolves*. Her stories and her teachings are enchanting, thought-provoking, soul-enriching, and exciting. She has given women a priceless gift.

### The Power Selves— Integrating the Gifts of the Inner Patriarch

On a more mundane note are the power selves within women that help to balance the Inner Patriarch's hold over us. The Inner Patriarch is always present. *When we do not have conscious access to his power, he will dominate us from the unconscious. When the Inner Patriarch dominates our lives from the unconscious, he makes us weak. Therefore, if we want to balance his power, we must learn from him; we must gain direct access to this power.* The basic lessons we must learn from him involve the ability to take care of ourselves in this world.

*The first lesson involves taking responsibility for ourselves, particularly financial responsibility.* Ask your Inner Patriarch; he knows how to do this. He worries a great deal about your financial security. That is one of the reasons why he is so eager for you to have a husband. He hopes that the man in your life will take care of you, both now and in the future. If you do not have access to your own Inner Patriarch's power in this area, look at the outer patriarchs, look at the men in your life who know how to take care of financial matters, and learn from them.

Your Inner Patriarch (or an outer one) can help you develop a self-sufficiency that will make you a more independent individual. He will probably begin by asking you all about your financial situation. He will want you to know about your current finances and about your plans for the future. If you do not know about this, he will insist that you find out. Do you know about your income, savings accounts, investments, home equity, loans, yearly expenditures? Have you enough income? Should you have more? Once you obtain this information, you can allow him to look at it objectively. He can help you evaluate your situation. Do you have enough information, or is this something you do not like to think about? If you're married, does your husband keep this kind of information to himself? Where is this information kept?

What arrangements have been made for medical insurance, life insurance, homeowners insurance, car insurance? What arrangements have been made for special expenditures such as vacations, your children's education, the purchase of a home, or your retirement? What happens if he cannot work? What happens if you cannot work? Your Inner Patriarch can advise you directly, or he can direct you to others for consultation.

*As you become knowledgeable and assume responsibility for your financial situation, you have a power that your Inner Patriarch can respect. If you are secure and certain, he will relax and give you the support you need.* He will no longer worry about you and question your ability to handle power in this area.

*The second lesson to learn from the Inner Patriarch is that of assuming authority. Listen to him, and use his energy when this is appropriate. The Inner Patriarch knows what he knows. He does not speak hesitantly. He does not ask others for permission. He says what he wants to say and does not worry about others' opinions.* Your ability to carry this authority will reassure him. The more you take this authority, the easier it becomes, but this is likely to take some time and practice. It is in this way, however, that you begin to integrate the energies of your Inner Patriarch and use him consciously. His power *becomes* yours rather than draining yours.

You will need to give yourself permission to take this step. Your Inner Patriarch has been telling you for your entire lifetime that you, as a woman, are not entitled to assume authority. You may need help from others to be able to take this power. Sometimes just having another person tell you that it is acceptable for you to speak out authoritatively will do. For others, it takes more. You have to find your own path. This often includes getting in touch with your own inner sources of authority through journaling, guided imagery, dreams, readings, or workshops.

*The third lesson has to do with objectivity, emotional availability, and setting boundaries.* We think of this as having the ability to be impersonal. Women have been trained to be personal—that is, to be essentially without boundaries: open, feeling, warm, and energetically available to others. The Inner Patriarch is not at all like this, and we women have an important lesson to learn from him. We do not want to go through life impersonally and objectively, but this is one of the lessons in power that it is imperative we learn. We need the ability to be impersonal when necessary.

The Inner Patriarch knows how to be impersonal, cool, and objective. He is a master at setting boundaries. He can evaluate a situation and interact with people impersonally and objectively. He can look at people with the same dispassionate objectivity that he might have for a mechanical problem. He does not get involved in feelings, although he can be quite present and available to others in his cool, objective fashion. This does not mean that he is necessarily cold, withdrawn, or walled off. It just means that he has boundaries; he is not always emotionally available.

Learning how to be impersonal when this is appropriate is extremely important. As you learn this lesson from your Inner Patriarch, or in classes, workshops, or therapy, you will find yourself able to separate gently from others and sit in a cooler space, one that is not always reactive to their needs and feelings. In the chapter on "Taking Command of Your Kingdom: Managing Your Energy Field," I will talk about this in more detail and will show you how to create energetic boundaries that will allow you to be impersonal and objective when you wish.

*The fourth lesson is one of focus and discipline.* The Inner Patriarch knows all about focusing upon a piece of work that he wants to do and disciplining himself to resist distractions in order to finish it. *He does not allow himself to be distracted by the needs or demands of others. What is important to him is his first priority. What comes forth from him is important. He naturally protects what is his, and he is eager to produce tangible results.* If you, as a woman, resist his demands for you to give the men and the children in your life first priority, and you do your own work, you will not only be integrating his energies and using them consciously, but eventually you will earn his grudging respect and support.

*The last lesson would be that of the righteous warrior.* The Inner Patriarch is a warrior. He will go to war if he feels that his rule or his kingdom is threatened. The women who led the feminist revolution of the past 30 years were not daughters; they were Amazon Warriors. They integrated this aspect of the Inner Patriarch's power in order to successfully battle the outer patriarchy. *Each woman needs to have some access to her own Warrior energy as one of the ways of integrating the Inner Patriarch's power and protecting her own kingdom.* Otherwise it is left up to the Inner Patriarch to protect it in the only ways that he knows how.

### The Goddesses or the Archetypal Selves

*Mythology gives us many archetypal selves that balance the Inner Patriarch by providing pictures of the sacred in female form. Every culture has its own myths; you can see which speak to you most directly.* Reading about these archetypal selves or goddesses helps us to incorporate their energies in our daily lives. Jean Shinoda Bolen has written an excellent, readable, and fascinating book called *Goddesses in Everywoman* that will introduce you to these archetypes as they appear in the Greek myths. These ancient symbols of aspects of the feminine can be used creatively in your own rituals, or in writing, art, music, dance, or in active imagination.

There are several ancient Greek goddesses who represent the traditionally feminine selves. These selves complement the Inner Patriarch; they balance him. They basically agree with his values and his requirements of women, and they conform to one or another of these requirements. We might think of them as the females who know how to dance with the Inner Patriarch.

The first of these, Hera, is the only married goddess on Olympus. She is married to Zeus, the chief of the gods. Her power comes to her through her marriage to the most powerful male, and not as a result of her own skills, efforts, or accomplishments. This way of gaining power is the ultimate goal of the Inner Patriarch. Hera is very much interested in this power and will do anything to hold on to it. She is intensely jealous of anyone who might disrupt the status quo. In mythology, Hera is not very happy, since she must tolerate the infidelities of her husband. Needless to say, she is not permitted any infidelities of her own. However, she knows the value of a strong male, and she fights to protect her power.

Then there is Hestia, the goddess of the hearth and home. She carries traditional feminine qualities and embodies all that is oriented to comfort and a safe, happy family life. However, she is a virgin goddess who has chosen not to be with a male. She balances the Inner Patriarch by allowing a woman to make a home independent of men, thus giving her dominion over her own life in a home-oriented, feminine fashion.

Of all the goddesses, Aphrodite is most like the traditionally feminine self. She is the goddess of beauty, attraction, and love. She is the epitome of feminine charm, of sensuality, and earthly love. She is the self that allows for sexuality, sensuality, and relationship. But she, even though she is feminine, expects to be honored and worshiped, never used. She becomes extremely vengeful if she feels that someone is trying to exploit her.

For the power selves, we have Kali, the supreme mother goddess of India in her negative aspect. Hers is the power of destruction. She destroys what she has created, and she gives us a bone-chilling picture of destructive female power as she smilingly dances upon the dead, wearing her necklace of human heads or drinking blood from a skull.

From the Western myths, we have Athena, a much more rational warrior. She sprang, fully formed, from the head of her father, Zeus. She is the goddess of wisdom, of strategy, of intrigue. She is a warrior. She does not become involved in relationship with men, but she knows how to talk with them and how to deal with them on their own terms. She has so much power of her own that the Inner Patriarch can depend upon her to take care of matters.

Artemis also carries power like the "natural woman." As a virgin goddess, she is not required to be with a man. Her power comes from being undomesticated, wild. She is a huntress and follows no rules but her own. She traditionally protects animals, virginity, and women in childbirth. She has great ability to make plans and carry them through without distraction. The Inner Patriarch can admire her qualities of objectivity and coolness although she is not at all subservient to men. Since she has access to her own power and is not unfeminine, however, he can relax when she is around.

All these goddesses can help you focus your efforts on balancing the power of your Inner Patriarch. Now let us move on to a consideration of who, or what, it is that can help you to move through life embracing these opposites.

# CHAPTER TWELVE

# BEYOND DUALITY—
# THE REALM OF THE AWARE EGO

*The Aware Ego is not a destination that can be
reached, but rather a process that must be lived.
It gives us more choices, more possibilities, more
directions in which to move.*

This chapter is about exploring a new dimension of consciousness, the realm of the Aware Ego. In it, I will talk about moving through life in a new way. This new way involves living life from an Aware Ego rather than from a primary self or selves. Hal and I chose the term *Aware Ego* to refer to the decision-making part of the psyche because the traditional term for this executive function has always been the *ego*. We wished to build upon the work of those who have preceded us and saw no reason to rid ourselves of this word. We also saw no reason to rid ourselves of the "ego," as many spiritual traditions teach. Instead, we believe that this original ego is included in the new Aware Ego.

### What Is the Aware Ego?

In most circles, when people talk about the ego, what they are really talking about are the primary selves that have dominated our lives and our ways of thinking. These selves are not really who we are, although we may think that they are. In the chapter on the Inner Patriarch, under the heading "The Inner Patriarch as One of our Many Selves," I described these primary selves. They are the dominant selves that take charge of us and our lives. They determine who we are, what we see, how we judge the world, how we think, and what we do. Therefore, they form our "operating ego"; they are the executives (or the committee in charge) of our psyche. Most of the time we do not give a lot of thought to how this operates. We simply go along, more or less trusting this operating ego's perceptions of the world, as if everything we see and feel and think about our surroundings is pretty much the way things are.

*All of us live our lives dominated by these highly developed primary selves. Sometimes they are very capable and they bring us success and happiness; sometimes they are less adaptive and they bring us pain or repeated frustrations and feelings of failure. Most primary selves do very well in some areas of our lives and less well in others.*

For instance, if I am a very hard worker and my primary selves are my Pusher (who knows how to work very hard) and my Perfectionist (who knows how to do things the right way), I will probably be very successful at my work. However, I will find it difficult to relax and enjoy myself and others. Every time I look at my husband, my children, or my friends, I think of things they could be doing or ways in which they could be improving themselves. I cannot just relax and enjoy who they are at this moment.

My Aware Ego is a new kind of ego. It is aware of these primary selves, but it is not identified with them or dominated by them. My Aware Ego takes advantage of what my Pusher and my Perfectionist have to offer, but it knows that there is more to life than what they see.

### Does This Mean That Up Until Now I Have Been Doing Things Wrong?

No! Absolutely not! There is nothing wrong with living from these primary selves. As a matter of fact, they deserve our heartfelt thanks. These are the selves that have made sense of the world around us and have taken care of us. We all have them, and just about all of us live lives dominated by them. Most of us are not aware of this fact, and we think that we have free choice; we think that we are consciously determining the course of our lives.

That is where the concept of an Aware Ego enters the picture. *As my Aware Ego awakens, I separate from my primary selves, and I literally become aware of the fact that it is they, not I, who have been living my life. My Aware Ego begins to take over this executive function and, as it stands between opposites, it begins to make the choices in my life. This does not mean that my life, up until now, has been a series of mistakes, though.*

## Beyond Duality

As my Aware Ego is awakened, however, I become aware of my Pusher, who is pressing down the accelerator of my psychological car even when it is stopped at the traffic light and my transmission is in neutral. I become aware of the fact that, as I sit on the porch enjoying the sunset with Hal, this Pusher is whispering in my ear: "How can you just sit there? You have a stack of letters on your desk that must be answered."

Simply because I am aware of this voice as a separate entity, it is at this point that I have moved from my original operating ego—that is, my Pusher, to an "Aware Ego." My Aware Ego combines the experience of the Pusher and her impatient demands with an "awareness" of this Pusher. This is why we call this new ego—which is separated from, but can experience and make use of, the information and experience of the selves (in this case, the Pusher)—the Aware Ego.

We define consciousness as being made up of three parts: the Aware Ego, the awareness (or witness), and the experience of the selves. You know about the selves already. The awareness is the witness state of unattached observation, insight, or meditation (the state pursued by many spiritual seekers). The Aware Ego moves through life using information from all these sources to arrive at its decisions.

Now let us return to the porch and my pressured Pusher. If my newly awakened Aware Ego is operating, it knows about the Pusher and can feel her anxiety, but it is not identified with this anxiety. In other words, it does not feel that the Pusher's demands must be acted upon; its view of life is not necessarily the only way to look at this situation. Therefore, I can look at the letters to be answered and know that there are selves within me that feel quite different from the way my Pusher does. This is where I can think about some of the balancing selves from the previous chapter. Perhaps this is a time to bring forth the Wife/Consort, the Being self, or Aphrodite. Any of these would tell me that the time on the porch watching the sunset with my husband is more important than answering the letters on my desk.

Whose views are correct? All of them are. Should I write the letters or not? What is the right thing to do? There is no "right" thing to do. This is where I have the opportunity to move beyond duality into the realm of the Aware Ego. As I stand between these two opposing views, knowing that they are both valid, I have a choice about how to behave. My Pusher has one set of suggestions; the other selves have other suggestions. I have a conflict, but I know that there is a way to move beyond this duality and make a choice that is based on these opposites.

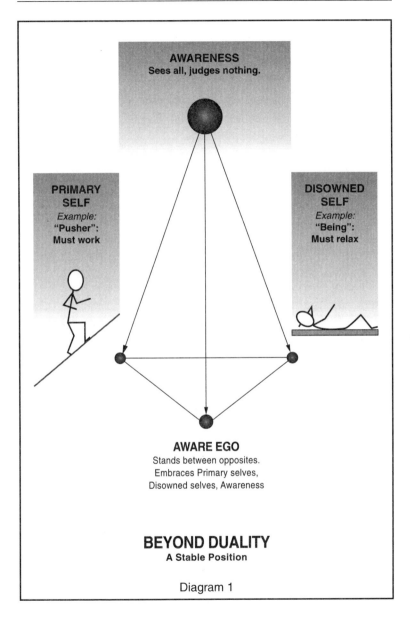

**AWARENESS**
Sees all, judges nothing.

**PRIMARY
SELF**
*Example:*
"Pusher":
Must work

**DISOWNED
SELF**
*Example:*
"Being":
Must relax

**AWARE EGO**
Stands between opposites.
Embraces Primary selves,
Disowned selves, Awareness

# BEYOND DUALITY
**A Stable Position**

Diagram 1

*An Aware Ego is amazingly creative. It can take both sides into consideration and come up with new solutions to previously insoluble problems. It is also capable of approaching the problem not as an either-or proposition, but more comprehensively, like a person taking suggestions from a group of consultants and then coming up with a solution that is a synthesis of them all, and not exactly like any single one. It moves us beyond dualistic thinking.*

Sometimes it can solve problems or make decisions immediately for something specific, such as my dilemma on the porch. Here it might mean taking a moment to schedule some time later in the evening or the next day for the letter writing so that my Pusher can relax, knowing that I have taken her concerns seriously. Then I can relax and continue to enjoy my time on the porch. That particular solution is fairly straightforward and simple.

What if, after considering both sides of this issue, it becomes apparent that the letters do need to be answered at this particular time, but that I also need to connect with my "Being" self (the self that can just sit and be rather than do) and with Hal as well? I must move beyond dualistic thinking and beyond duality to handle this challenge.

Fortunately, the Aware Ego exists in a realm that is beyond duality, and it can literally contain opposites. Our individual selves cannot do this. My Pusher cannot make contact with Hal; that is not what she does. My Pusher is not involved in emotional interactions; she is a worker and quite proud of that fact. In contrast, my Being self cannot write letters; she is incapable of doing focused work. If we return to the porch once more, what might my Aware Ego do to contain these obviously irreconcilable opposites? What would this look like or, better yet, what would it feel like?

My Aware Ego would take the time to make a lovely "being" connection, or an energetic linkage, with my husband. This is an energetic connection that I (or, more properly speaking, my Aware Ego) can maintain even while I am in the next room writing letters. This is a connection that we sometimes make automatically when we first fall in love or when we have children. We can be in another room, or another building, even in another city or country, and we do not lose an essential contact with them.

It is only possible for me to maintain this kind of energetic linkage with Hal while I am working on a task when I am operating beyond duality; in this example, if my Aware Ego writes the letters rather than my Pusher. When my Pusher writes the letters, I have no connection to anyone; I am just "doing." *The trick, therefore, is to maintain a connection to both sets of selves, to balance the opposites as I work.*

### Balancing Opposites—Walking on Two Feet

Picture me trying to get through life using only one foot. Think of my Pusher as my right foot. I could try to get through life hopping along on only that. Conversely, my Being self would be my left foot. I could abandon my Pusher and try to get through life with only my Being self. If I did that, I would be hopping on my left foot. *Right foot or left foot, either one is awkward, and I am unstable and easily pushed over or tipped. My Aware Ego moves through life between opposites, or using both feet. I am steadier and more balanced. I can walk over rough terrain without losing my balance, and others cannot push me over easily.*

How might I walk on two feet while I work? How might my Aware Ego maintain awareness of, and contact with, these opposites? I might, in this instance, play some music and/or light incense to make the letter writing a more soulful experience. This takes care of my Being self as I go about my letter writing so that my Pusher does not take over this task (which it will most definitely try to do). On the other hand, I could get carried away by the incense, the music, and my Being self. If that happens, I have merely switched from hopping on my right foot to hopping on my left foot. I am still not using both feet to help me move through life. If my Being self takes over, I will lose the connection to my

Pusher and be unable to write at all. My Aware Ego contains the opposites, it uses both feet, and can maintain all these connections simultaneously. *Sometimes this is effortless, but at other times there is great discomfort.*

### Enter the Inner Patriarch—The Dualistic Perspective

The Inner Patriarch is dualistic and has very little patience with this kind of thinking. *The basic patriarchal view is as follows: there is a right way to do things and a wrong way.* Either my Pusher was right or it was wrong. If it was right, then why should I take the trouble to awaken an Aware Ego? It would be best to just keep going along as I have in the past. I will certainly get a great deal accomplished. If, on the other hand, my Pusher was not right, then I should just change the way that I behave and accept the fact that I have been wrong for the past 59 years. However, I must admit that this idea that I have been doing things wrong is very upsetting to both my Pusher and my Inner Patriarch. Neither of them likes to make mistakes. Unfortunately, mistakes are an inevitable part of their dualistic thinking!

There is one other role that the Inner Patriarch plays in our attempts to awaken our Aware Egos and to stand between opposites. Our Inner Patriarch carries a set of rules and values that affect us whether or not we know about them. What might this look like?

Let us return once more to the porch at sunset, and to my conflict. If we look carefully, we can discern another player in my little drama. This player, however, operates in the shadows. My Inner Patriarch, operating from my unconscious, might agree with my Pusher. After all, my Inner Patriarch values work that is tangible, and he has little patience with relaxation and enjoyment unless, of course, I am recuperating from an illness. He would tilt the balance and send me off to answer letters. metaphorically hopping on my right foot.

On the other hand, my Inner Patriarch might take the opposite point of view, ally with my Being self, and emphasize the importance of taking care of my husband. In that case, he would lecture me on the importance of my relationship and urge me to relax, sit still, pay attention to Hal, and forget about my letter writing. This, of course would be very difficult for my Pusher, but I might do so anyway because the Inner Patriarch is very convincing. If this happens, I am (metaphorically) hopping on my left foot; I stay on the porch, and I do nothing about the letters. Then after I have spent some time on the porch tending the relationship just like he told me to, my Inner Patriarch would have no respect for what I had produced. The letters are still unanswered. No wonder these Inner Patriarchs can drive us wild! Sometimes it seems as though we're damned if we do and damned if we don't.

If I do not know about this Inner Patriarch and his values, my Aware Ego does not have access to this information and cannot add it into the process. However, if I have done my homework and I do know about my Inner Patriarch and his values, my Aware Ego can add this knowledge into its data bank and work with this information as well, making choices with very little effort and far fewer negative repercussions. What happens when I do not know about this Inner Patriarch?

## The Shadow King—
### When the Inner Patriarch Operates from the Unconscious

Let us return to the porch once again. This time, the scenario is different. It is early evening, and Hal and I are sitting quietly, watching the deer drink from our small pond. We are resting peacefully after having worked in the garden together. Our Being selves are enjoying life. We stay this way for some time. Then, gradually, I find myself getting ready to move on to something else. But I continue to sit.

I have not written all day because I felt that it was time to take a break, but I had been enjoying my writing the day before. As we sit quietly, I begin to think of this book. An idea comes to me. It is a good idea, and I would love to write it down while it is still fresh in my mind. But I feel a bit guilty about ending this lovely interlude, so I continue to sit where I am. By now, I am becoming somewhat restless, but still I do not move. I seem to be waiting for something, but I do not know what it is.

Why can't I move? What is keeping me here? There is something happening beyond my awareness in my unconscious. I have a primary self operating, but it is a self that operates unconsciously. This is not like my Pusher, which is also a primary self, but one that operates consciously. I always know what my Pusher is saying. My Pusher is accessible, conscious, and outspoken. I often hear myself using her favorite expressions, such as: "This will only take a minute more" or "I'll feel so much better if I just finish this."

The Inner Patriarch is different. I cannot access his thoughts so easily. If I could tune in to him at this moment, I would hear him say something like: "You cannot leave your husband at a lovely moment like this. You cannot abandon him for your own selfish interests. That is not the way a good wife behaves. A good wife waits until her husband is ready to move on. She lets him set the pace." These are some of his rules about relationships. But I am not aware of him at this moment. My Inner Patriarch is unconscious, and I am the good daughter obeying his rules. I am stuck in my chair until Hal decides to leave.

If this delay takes long enough, I well may change from good daughter to bad daughter. Even though I continue to sit still, I begin to resent Hal because he has not given me permission to leave and begin to write. I may even feel that he is deliberately keeping me from doing the work that I really want to do. I can continue to sit still until I get really angry and become rebellious. Then I leave the porch in full rebellion against his inconsiderate ways. Unfortunately, Hal does not know about any of this. It is all going on inside of me. This interaction is basically between me and my (unconscious) Inner Patriarch.

But let us assume that I know about my Inner Patriarch and the ways in which he can dominate my thoughts from the unconscious. I have some separation from him, and I am operating from an Aware Ego. I have an awareness that something is going on and, since I am behaving like a daughter instead of a grown woman, it probably has something to do with my Inner Patriarch. I have a sense that I am following a rule, and I wonder what the rule is. I tune in and discover the rule: "A good wife waits until her husband is ready to move on. She lets him set the pace."

My Aware Ego can contain these opposites. It can hold the Inner Patriarch's requirement that I must honor my relationship and my need to write, both at the same time. It can move freely, checking out the reality rather than my Inner Patriarch's interpretation of the situation. My Aware Ego can maintain contact with another person (like Hal) and his wishes and still make an independent decision about what to do next.

There is another very practical aspect to becoming aware of my Inner Patriarch and bringing his operations from the shadows of my unconscious into the light of consciousness. I can ask Hal how he feels, rather than automatically listening to my Inner Patriarch's version of how he feels. Maybe Hal does want us to remain together for a while. If so, I must weigh this against my own needs. Perhaps, on the other hand, Hal is just waiting for me to leave the porch so he would not hurt my feelings, and each of us has been waiting for the other. Perhaps he really likes to hear me working at my computer and would prefer that I write for a while because this makes him feel good. It is even possible that at this moment he does not care what I do. Obviously, I will never know until I ask.

### The Realm of the Aware Ego

*As you can see, moving beyond a dualistic view of the world gives me more information, greater flexibility, and balance. It literally lowers my center of gravity and makes me more stable. If I spend my life in du-*

ality, I can be tossed between opposites, as if I were on a seesaw. When I have all the weight on my side, with my primary selves in charge, I can keep you up in the air. But if you can manage to sit on the opposite side and add a bit of weight to my disowned selves, you can flip me up into the air and keep me there. I lose all my power. Basically I am identified with one side of the seesaw (perhaps being unselfish), and I have disowned the opposite (selfish) and made it wrong.

This provides a graphic picture of how I can be tipped from one side to another. But there is another way to ride a seesaw. Have you ever stood in the middle of an empty seesaw with a foot on either side? It is a great sensation that is at the very edge where movement and balance meet. You are in charge of both sides simultaneously; you are responding to very slight changes, and you can move between the opposites as you please.

What does this tossing between opposites look like when I am interacting with someone who has a different primary self from mine? For example, let us assume that I am monogamous and you are not. You tell me that this is a foolish way to live. If I live in duality, my primary self, not my Aware Ego, has made this decision. I am hopping on one foot, my "monogamous" foot. I can either agree with what you have said and feel foolish, or I can disagree with you, decide that you are the foolish one, and feel self-righteous. Either way, my situation is not a stable one. Your comment has upset my equilibrium. We can no longer be mutually respectful friends.

But if my Aware Ego is operating, I am aware of the yearnings of my Aphrodite as well as the cautions of my Inner Patriarch. I am moving through life with an arm around each. I have already dealt with this conflict inside of myself, so I am not surprised by your reaction to my way of life. I am not thrown off balance by your statement that my decision to live a monogamous life is a foolish one. I know that there is a part of me that agrees with you totally, but, nonetheless, this is what I have decided to do. I am walking on two feet, not hopping on one; I am riding the center of the seesaw. My equilibrium is not upset, and I have no need to make you wrong in order to maintain my position.

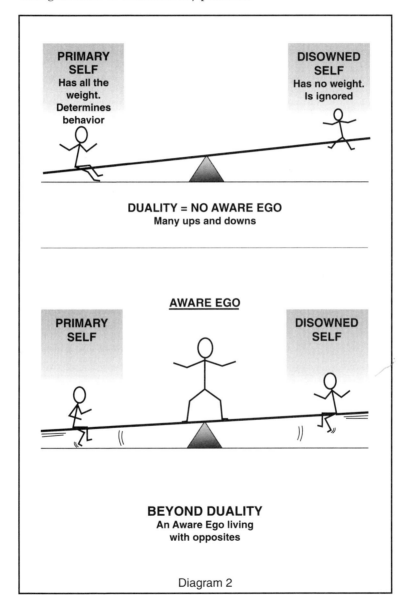

Diagram 2

Through the Aware Ego, I can walk the edge between chaos and form and maintain my equilibrium. There is a magnificent description of this in Michael Crichton's book, *Lost Worlds*:

> ...*Complex systems seem to strike a balance between the need for order and the imperative to change. Complex systems tend to locate themselves at a place we call "the edge of chaos." We imagine the edge of chaos as a place where there is enough innovation to keep a living system vibrant, and enough stability to keep it from collapsing into anarchy. It is a zone of conflict and upheaval, where the old and the new are constantly at war. Finding the balance point must be a delicate matter. If a living system drifts too close to chaos, it risks falling over into incoherence and dissolution; but if the system moves too far from the edge, it becomes rigid, frozen, totalitarian. Both conditions lead to extinction. Too much change is as destructive as too little. Only at the edge of chaos can complex systems flourish.*

This realm of the Aware Ego is kinetic rather than static; it is constantly in movement. It takes the concerns of the Inner Patriarch into consideration and moves with them in new and exciting ways. The Aware Ego is not a destination that can be reached, but rather a process that must be lived. It gives us more choices, more possibilities, more directions in which to move. We no longer deal in "either/or"; instead we are able to think in terms of "and." We can move through lives like jugglers or dancers. What we are juggling or dancing with are energies—and that is the subject of the next chapter.

# TAKING COMMAND
# OF YOUR KINGDOM—
# MANAGING YOUR ENERGY FIELD

*For millennia we women have been taught to be
energetically open to the world, to be personal
and accepting. We have been trained to move
through life with an open energy field, to blend with
the people in our lives who are important to us.*

In the last chapter, I talked about how the Aware Ego gives us
a new way to move through life. Once we make these changes
and begin to open up to the world beyond the clearly mecha-
nistic and dualistic one that we have been inhabiting, we think of
life differently, and we look for new theories to explain how the
world works. We look at the repetitive patterns that exist in
chaotic and seemingly unrelated situations, as in the Chaos the-
ory. We move beyond a simple consideration of cause and effect,
or causal thinking, and add to this the idea of synchronicity (or co-
incidence) where two events that are not necessarily causally con-
nected are, nevertheless, related. Time, space, and energy are not
as clearly differentiated as they used to be.

*The skills that I would like to address in this chapter are the ones you
need in order to be able to manage your own energy fields. These skills
are another method for bringing your authority back home to you and
away from undue outside influences.* The Inner Patriarch concen-
trates upon externally imposed rules and requirements because he

basically does not trust internal personal impulse control. This is sometimes necessary, but it tends to encourage women to give away dominion over themselves. Taking over the control of your energies and your energy fields both reassures the Inner Patriarch (because you have taken responsibility for yourself) and lessens his power (because he is no longer needed to protect you in the same way).

### What Are the Body Energy Fields?

The knowledge of the body's energy fields is an ancient one. For millennia, traditional Chinese doctors have focused upon these energy systems within the body. They see this body energy, or "chi," as moving through our bodies along what they call the "energy meridians" much like our blood runs through the circulatory system or our neural impulses travel along the pathways of the nervous system. They work with the chi, balancing these energy meridians and treating blockages with acupuncture and other energy-based healing medications and technology. Once the chi flows freely again, the body is able to regain its natural balance and function smoothly. Our energy fields are not limited to the boundaries of our physical bodies, however.

*When I talk about our energy fields, I am talking about the energies that extend beyond our physical bodies and are usually invisible to the naked eye.* We can see our physical bodies because the energy of our physical body vibrates at a rate that can be detected by our eyes. We can see the colors red or blue in the visible spectrum in much the same way; the vibrational frequency of red or blue can be detected by the mechanisms that operate in our eyes. The part of our energy fields that extends beyond the body is different, however. It is like the infrared or ultraviolet light, or like x-rays. Most of us cannot see them with the naked eye, but they are vibrating energies, nonetheless, and you can experience the effects that they have on your body.

There are some people who can see these energy fields that extend outward from our bodies and some newly developed instruments that are now taking pictures of them. We all experience these energy fields, however, even if we do not know about them. We feel the warmth of someone whose energy field is touching ours or the coolness of someone whose energies are withdrawn from us. We may not have words for this, but the sensations are well known to us.

I am sure that you have had the experience of having somebody move into your energy field and making you uncomfortable. When this happens, you feel as though the other person is standing too close to you, and you are uneasy; you want that person to move. Sometimes that person is not even physically close; perhaps he is standing across the room, but you feel invaded anyway. This means that he has extended his energy field until it is actually touching or entering yours. He may be doing this deliberately, or he may have no awareness of what he is doing and how invasive this is.

There are other times when you've probably had the opposite experience; these are the times when someone is talking to you and you feel lonesome, as though nobody is there. This means that the other person's energies are not with you; they are elsewhere. For instance, somebody says "I love you," and you feel depressed rather than delighted. Something is missing. The words are right, but the energy that accompanies them is all wrong. There is no energetic linkage to tell you that this person is really with you and truly loves you.

There have always been people who know about these energies. Great entertainers have always been masters of their energy fields. When they perform, they move different energies (or subpersonalities) in and out as needed. They can extend their energy fields so that you can feel them even at the back of a huge amphitheater. Many of the martial arts, with Aikido as the foremost amongst these, train their practitioners to use these energies for both protection and power.

179

Hal is known for his pioneering work on the role that these energy fields play in our lives, our relationships, and our health. The exercises that I will present to you are part of a series of exercises that he has evolved over the years. These teach people how to manage the energy fields that surround them.

### Setting Boundaries

For millennia, we women have been taught to be energetically open to the world, to be personal and accepting. We have been trained to move through life with an open energy field, to blend with the people in our lives who are important to us. Everyone "knows" that it is feminine to be receptive and available, to be able to interact smoothly and pleasantly with other people and to blend our energies with theirs. The Inner Patriarch is very enthusiastic about this. He does not like women who are unavailable energetically.

*As women, it is important for us to have some awareness of our own energy fields and to have real choice in whether or not they are open. Men have been trained to set boundaries, to be objective, to be self-contained. They know how to define their own energetic space and reality. We women may have learned how to be self-contained or objective when at work, but most of us do not have this quality available to us at home or in our relationships.*

There are several ways to begin to develop this quality in yourself. Take a few moments and sit quite still. Picture a shining core running down your spine, and extend energy from this core like a golden light. Feel it contain you comfortably and easily, not harshly or defensively. You are now surrounded gently by your own energy field. It has an outer edge, but it does not wall you off from others; it just separates you softly so that you can see them and be with them, but you are not blending with them. Think of yourself and the other person like colors in a painting. These colors do not run together, but there is no harsh black outline that separates them.

The two colors have been painted side by side, and each one remains distinct.

Another image to use when training yourself to contain your own energy field is to picture a woman who does this well, and use her for a model. Both Katharine Hepburn and Meryl Streep have carried this impersonal self-contained energy without losing their femininity. It is as though they carry with them an automatic set of boundaries that say quite clearly: "You may come this far and not any further until I invite you to do so." This is neither a challenge nor a punishment, but a simple statement of fact.

There are times when a simple separation of this sort is not enough. There are people in this world who are energy masters and who will try to move into your space. Whether they are doing this deliberately or unconsciously, it is important for you to have the ability and to take the authority to move them out at your own discretion. Your physical body is yours, and the energetic area surrounding you is yours as well. This is your domain, and you should be the ultimate authority on who is permitted to enter it.

For these times when a simple boundary is not enough, practice something stronger. Picture yourself turning a dial that allows you to intensify this energy field around you. You can make it as impenetrable as you wish. You can make it stronger or thicker. You can add color if that helps.

### Creating an Energy Shield

As a final protection of your energy field, you can surround it with a shield of your own creation. You initially create this shield through imagery, but you can draw it, paint it, sculpt it, or build if you wish to give it added dimensionality. Again, take time when you can be alone and will not be interrupted. Now sit down quietly and take a few deep breaths to relax. Feel the core energy within you and the surrounding energy field. Now picture a shield that surrounds your entire energy field and protects you. This shield should be egg shaped and surround you completely, with plenty of room for you to move your arms and legs within it. If you wish, you can create extra protection over your heart and your pelvic area or any other place where you might feel vulnerable.

You can create your shield of pure energy, or you can use crystal, light, metal, stone, torrents of running water, whatever you wish. It can be any color or texture. It can have designs that are meaningful to you, or it can be plain. It can have movement over its surface, or it can be still. Whatever it is, it is yours alone, and you can call it forth whenever you feel this is necessary. Just picture it to yourself, and feel it reappear. Practice sometime. Just picture your shield and move it outward toward someone else, perhaps someone in line next to you at the supermarket. It is very likely that the other person will move a bit away from you. Some people are visual and can picture this easily; others are more kinesthetic and will feel it. Some people can even add sounds or aromas to the shield. Add as much as you personally can to make yours as strong as possible. It is important that you have the choice to use this.

Once we are able to do this, our Inner Patriarchs can relax even further. They can trust in our ability to know ourselves clearly and independently of those around us. They can trust that we have learned to set our own boundaries and they no longer need to work so hard to protect us from the world.

### Energetic Linkage

Now that you have learned how to separate your energy field from someone else's, it is time to learn how to do the opposite. There are times when it is very important to establish what we call an "energetic linkage" or a blending of the energy fields. *We see this energetic linkage between two people as one of the most precious components of a fulfilling relationship. It gives a kind of intimacy that we yearn for, an intimacy that is only available with this kind of energetic connection.*

In the past, these energetic linkages were unconscious. We women did not have a choice about them. Our Inner Patriarchs felt that our relationships were extremely important and that there were many rules for creating and then maintaining them. Some of these rules, I might point out, are pretty much on target. They work! As I've said before, the Inner Patriarch's rules should not be thoughtlessly discarded in rebellion and anger any more than they should be unquestioningly followed with humble docility. One set of these rules is about energetic linkage.

*We women have traditionally been taught to allow our energy fields to blend with those of others. We were expected to be open and energetically available. We were not permitted to keep other people's energies out. When we allowed this linkage unconsciously, we did not know where we ended and someone else began. We felt the other person's feelings. We lost our identities, we merged with others, we fused, we became co-dependent.* As this lack of energetic boundaries was discovered, it was called pathology, and we were told by the experts that all such linkage was bad. We were warned to avoid it at all costs.

Energetic linkage is not bad, but it is not always good either. What we need is the ability to choose when and where it is appropriate for us. For instance, if a mother does not link energetically with an infant, the child will probably not thrive. If we do not link energetically with our loved ones, we feel alone and do not know what is bothering us. We yearn for something more in our relationships, but we may not know what it is.

*This linkage is not just for romantic relationships, you can achieve it anytime or anyplace. Very often it is the ineffable aspect of a very special encounter that stays with you for a lifetime.* For instance, I remember one day many years ago, 34 to be exact, when I was shopping in Altman's coat department in New York City. I was a young mother, and I had my infant daughter with me. The saleswoman was a very ordinary woman, about 30 years older than I, but there was something different about our contact with her. She looked at both of us; she really looked at us, and I could feel her energetic presence there with me.

Although what we spoke about was the purchase of a particular coat, in our contact this saleswoman gave me the gift of herself. In this process, she gave me the gift of myself as well. She was fully present. I could feel the energy that was distinctly hers, which was self-aware, understanding, warm, and a bit wistful, as though in looking at me she could see the part of her life that was past. There was a sweetness and a sadness about her. As her energies linked with mine, I could feel not only her, but myself and the energy that was distinctly mine as well. I could feel the newness of being a mother and a psychologist, the excitement of my life and just a touch of fear that all these good things might vanish like a dream. This unknown saleswoman and I linked energetically and, in that interchange, she gave me the permission to enjoy all this and to trust it for as long as it would last. There was the sense that it was all fleeting, although this idea, too, was never verbalized.

This interchange was so ordinary, and at the same time so extraordinary, that I spoke about it to a neighbor several weeks later when she admired my new coat. This neighbor was astonished. She recognized the woman I described as her much-loved maiden aunt who sold coats at Altman's. This aunt had never had children, but all the children in the family knew there was something special about her, and they loved her. Although we did not think in terms of energetic linkages in those days, this woman had the gift of making an energetic linkage with other human beings and, in doing this, of giving them a sense of themselves. Also, without words, she could communicate energetically. The sweet sadness that I had sensed was that she was dying. By the time I spoke with my neighbor, this remarkable and totally ordinary woman had died of cancer. I have often wondered how many other people's lives were changed by her gift of energetic linkage.

### How Do We Create This Energetic Linkage?

*Energy follows thought. If you think or visualize the movement of your energy field, it will happen.* You do have to relax, however. This is not one of those areas in which extra effort helps. Of course, it is best to be introduced to the body energy fields and to energetic linkage by someone who is already familiar with this concept. However, if nobody is available to teach you, there are ways to learn about this without an experienced teacher. I am going to suggest some exercises that you can do.

The actual practice of energetic linkage must be done with a partner. You cannot link with another person unless there is someone there. This does not have to be someone with whom you have a deep relationship, just someone who is open to these ideas. Sit facing your partner with your knees about a foot apart. You do not want your bodies to be touching. You do want room for the air to flow between you.

Take a few breaths and relax. Know that you are surrounded by an energy field, and allow this field to be natural. Now picture (or feel) the core of energy running down the center of your body. Picture or feel the field of energy that extends from this core and surrounds you. Energy follows thought. You will use your thoughts or your visualizations to control this field just as you did in the section of this chapter on setting boundaries.

In this exercise, you will alternate between linking energetically and withdrawing energetically. First allow your energy field to expand and to blend with the person opposite you. You can talk while you're doing this; you do not have to remain silent if this is not comfortable. Allow yourself to feel the delicious warmth of this connection. You like this person, and it is lovely to connect energies in this way.

*Please note:* For some people, this kind of closeness is not warm or delicious; it is not even comfortable. If you are one of these peo-

185

ple for whom energetic linkage is truly uncomfortable, and if this does not feel good to you, then withdraw your energies and do not continue this exercise. You might even decide to investigate why this sort of closeness is so painful for you.

To continue with the exercise, nobody is expected to remain in close energetic linkage forever. Now it is time to withdraw. You are exercising your right of free choice. You have decided that this is too much closeness and intimacy. Withdraw your energies consciously. Pull them back close around you. You need your own space. Create it. Enjoy it. Experience the energetic vacuum between you and your partner. See how this feels to you.

Now decide that you have had enough separation, and allow your energies to mingle with your partner's once again. Link energetically with your partner. Feel the closeness and the warmth. Is this more comfortable for you, or did you prefer the separation? Alternate between this linkage and the separation of energies until you get a clear sense of the difference and you feel an ability to control your field.

Now you can take turns with your partner, and try variations on this exercise. One of you can hold a boundary, or shield yourself, while the other tries to invade energetically. The stronger the invading energy, the stronger is your resistance. Can you push the other person out? Work at this until you're able to do so.

Try something entirely different. Picture your field extending and filling up the room. See what it's like to take command of an entire space. Have your partner indicate when he or she feels this happen. Picture yourself withdrawing until you're very, very small and have your partner indicate when he or she feels this.

### An Alternative Image

Again, sit facing your partner with your knees about a foot apart. Picture a dial near your hand, one that you can turn, that will control the energies in your vicinity. Have your partner gradually beam stronger and stronger energies toward you. The person who is beaming these energies should not do anything sudden because you are both learning how to handle the energy field between you. As these energies become intense, instead of trying to push them out, just use your dial to turn them down. Conversely, if you wish to increase the intensity and/or extent of the energy field between you and allow a more intense energetic linkage, turn your dial up.

Now, reverse the procedure and you send energy, using your dial or whatever image works for you. You can use this imaginary dial to work with your own energies. Turn it up to intensify them or to extend them, and turn them down to weaken them or draw them back toward you. Use whatever images work for you. You might even wish to create new ones. Your partner will now use his or her dial to manage the energies that you are sending.

As you do these exercises, give each other feedback; let one another know what you experience. Mutually check out your perceptions of the extent and the intensity of your energy fields. How far out do they extend? Are they strong or weak? Learn from one another. Gradually become more and more comfortable with this way of experiencing the world. You have been experiencing this all through your life, but until you bring some awareness to what is going on, this is all happening unconsciously and without choice.

Sometimes it can be fun to move beyond a partner and to play with these energy fields a bit to get an additional sense of how they work. Give someone a gift, a gift that he or she does not know about. Pick someone in your surroundings, perhaps a waitress in a restaurant who is looking harassed, or a tired person working behind a checkout counter in a store. Picture a beam of loving energy streaming out from your heart and surrounding this individual. Feel the warmth as the energy travels from you to this other person. Do not say anything; just let your energies blend. Wait for a few minutes, and see if this person's facial expression changes. You do not have to be close to the other person to do this.

As you move into your daily life with this knowledge about yourself, your Inner Patriarch, and your energy field, you will probably see your surroundings in a different light and notice that this information is all quite practical and empowering

## The Goal Is Mastery of Your Own Domain

In reading this book, you have seen how much the Inner Patriarch, the Shadow King, has been ruling women from the shadows of the unconscious. Once we shine the light of awareness into these shadows and see and hear what is happening, his power lessens. We listen to what he has to say, and we can evaluate it. We become familiar with his rules, and now have choice about these rules and about his advice. We can agree or we can disagree. We can do what we need to do to address his basic anxiety about our safety. We can use balancing selves or energies as we see fit.

The goal of all this is to gain mastery over our own domain. The exercises in this chapter add yet another dimension to this mastery. They enable us to control our own energy fields and to make a choice between separating our energy fields from someone else's and blending with that other person.

Mastery of these energy fields also provides access to an entirely new kind of intimacy, the intimacy of the Aware Ego. In the past, intimacy has been seen as two people being open and blending energy fields. There are no boundaries available and no choices possible, only the flowing together of the two energy fields. There is no consciousness or awareness, just the experience of being together in this way. The intimacy of the Aware Ego is different , but it does contain this experience of blending energies. From the Aware Ego we can consciously move back and forth between these opposites while we maintain a basic energetic linkage with another person—that is, we can either enjoy a full energetic blending of energies, or we can re-establish our boundaries and separate our energies.

When we do have these choices and we exercise them consciously, our Inner Patriarch can relax his demands that we defer to the powerful people of the world. We have taken charge of our own energy fields, and we are the rightful rulers of our own kingdoms. He no longer requires us to exchange our own authority in return for the external protection provided by men. The Shadow King no longer rules us.

Once we have this authority and we are no longer daughters to our Inner Patriarchs, they begin to support us from within as a strong masculine energy that is ours to depend upon and to enjoy. We can be powerful and separate without having sacrificed our ability to be intimate and energetically linked through an Aware Ego. Men recognize that we are self-sufficient and are with them because we want to be with them. At the same time, they can see that we have not sacrificed any of our femininity. We are now in a position to be full partners to both our Inner Patriarchs and to the men in our lives.

# BREAKING THE ENCHANTMENT

*The Inner Patriarch acts like the magician in the fairy tales, transforming a grown woman into a daughter. This daughter, in turn, transforms every man that she meets into a father and so subverts her own power. Through the New Woman's vision, we rewrite this fairy tale. With the Aware Ego and our newly found Feminine Power, we women can break the enchantment that has held us, and the men in our lives, captive for so long.*

As I envision the evolution of our present civilization, I see women transforming themselves consciously and taking the next step forward in full, mutually respectful partnership with men. This would be neither a matriarchal society nor a patriarchal society, but one in which both men and women, and their respective gifts, would be equally valued.

If we women wish to have an impact on the world today, we cannot destroy all that has come before. We must work with the concerns of our Inner Patriarchs; we must be discerning, not dismissive, when we look at the values and traditions that they carry. *Once they know that we are aware of their underlying concerns, capable of assuming full responsibility for ourselves, and able to work cooperatively with them, the enchantment is broken.* Our Inner Patriarchs become valued partners and offer their own special kind of support and protection from within.

*Any major change in consciousness involves moving beyond our current dualistic approach to life.* When it comes to transforming ourselves, this means embracing our power as women while we continue to carry within us and honor the values and gifts of the patriarchal tradition that have brought us this far in our journey. We will consciously embrace the power of a very dynamic set of opposite selves: the Inner Patriarch and the Woman of Feminine Power. What emerges is the image of the New Woman, the woman that we want ourselves, our daughters, and our granddaughters to be.

As we move beyond duality and hold the tension of these opposites, that is, the tension between our need for the full expression of our female power and the fears of the Inner Patriarch, we are able to take the next step in our conscious evolution as women of power. As we embrace opposites, others will learn to do so as well. As we hold the tension of these opposites within ourselves, we will be able to expand our vision to include the world outside of us, a world torn apart by a dualistic approach to life that divides human beings into conflicting groups.

The Inner Patriarch acts like the magician in the fairy tales, transforming a grown woman into a daughter. This daughter, in turn, transforms every man that she meets into a father and so subverts her own power. Through the New Woman's vision, we rewrite this fairy tale. With the Aware Ego and our newly found Feminine Power, we women can break the enchantment that has held us, and the men in our lives, captive for so long.

We as women have brought about many changes in ourselves and our surroundings during these past three decades and will bring forth even more changes in the future. Our job—now that we have faced the outer patriarchs, and in many instances have enlisted their aid—is to face our Inner Patriarchs and to enlist *their* help.

*Our Inner Patriarchs are being awakened to the fact that we women are born with the necessary power, objectivity, and skills to not only survive, but excel, in today's world.* They finally see that what we women can produce both professionally and in the home are equally important and should be valued as such. The true significance of childbearing and childrearing for the survival of humanity will be appreciated. And as this occurs, men will be freed from their enchantment and come to value their own importance in this process.

As we free ourselves from the enchantment of our own Inner Patriarchs, our Shadow Kings, we will no longer project their power upon the men around us and cause these men to polarize against us and our ideas. In this way, our transformation can free the men from the tyranny of *their* Patriarchs within and move them forward in their own transformational process.

When we are daughters, the men in our lives can only be our fathers. When we avoid men, they cannot be with us at all. When we come to them in the totality of our beings as women, including both our strength and our sensitivity, we are free to partner one another as peers. It is my vision that in this way, men and women, as full and equal partners, will be able to consciously co-create a new civilization, one in which the traditionally feminine contributions are equal in importance to those that are traditionally masculine, and that our full human birthright is restored.

**Sidra Stone, Ph.D.,** is a clinical psychologist, an internationally recognized author, teacher, and psychotherapist. She is the cocreator, with her husband and partner, Hal Stone, Ph.D., of Voice Dialogue, an exciting and powerful method for exploring our many selves. Together, they have co-authored the bestselling books *Embracing Our Selves, Embracing Each Other,* and *Embracing Your Inner Critic*. As a woman who has lived through six decades of dramatic changes in women's roles—as a professional woman; and as a mother, stepmother, and grandmother—she is particularly interested in issues that affect women. She currently lives in Mendocino County on the mystical, fog-shrouded coast of Northern California.

For information about trainings, workshops, and individual consultations, or to purchase books and tapes, contact:

Delos, Inc., P.O. Box 604, Albion, CA 95410-0604
Phone: 707-937-2424  Fax: 707-937-4119
E-mail: delos@mcn.org  Website: http://delos-inc.com/


## N  A  T  A  R  A  J
## P  U  B  L  I  S  H  I  N  G

is committed to acting as a catalyst for change and transformation in the world by providing books and tapes on the leading edge in the fields of personal and social consciousness growth. *Nataraj* is a Sanskrit word referring to the creative, transformative power of the universe. For more information on our company, please contact us at:

Nataraj Publishing, P.O. Box 2430, Mill Valley, CA 94942
Phone: (415) 388-7195
E-mail: nataraj@nataraj.com  Website: http://www.nataraj.com

# BOOKS AND AUDIOCASSETTES FROM NATARAJ PUBLISHING

## Books

*Awakening the Warrior Within.* By Dawn Callan. This is like no other book you will ever read. It explodes contemporary myths about attaining personal safety, revealing how those myths may actually contribute to our victimization. More important, it tells how we can enjoy unparalleled levels of security and inner strength—even in a world where physical, emotional, and spiritual abuse are escalating. (Tradepaper $12.95)

*Awakening: A Daily Guide to Conscious Living.* By Shakti Gawain. Shakti has written a daily meditation guide that focuses on maintaining our spiritual center when we are in solitude, as well as when we are active in the world. In these daily entries, Shakti explores how to live universal principles every day, accepting and balancing the many aspects of ourselves, living with the dualities and polarities of life, and exploring our inner shadow. (Tradepaper $9.95)

*Coming Home: The Return to True Self.* By Martia Nelson. The author presents a clear and inspiring explanation of how we can integrate our human experience with our essential spiritual nature and express the potential that dwells in each of us. You'll receive guidance on living from the perspective of our soul, while also honoring the needs of our personality. *Coming Home* is the guidebook for returning meaning, passion, and purpose to your life. (Tradepaper $12.95)

*Corporate Renaissance: Business as an Adventure in Human Development.* By Rolf Osterberg. Bestselling Swedish author and successful businessman Rolf Osterberg explodes the myth that a business' greatest asset is capital. Osterberg presents the revolutionary idea that "the purpose of a company is to serve as an arena for the personal and human development of the people working in the company." (Hardcover $18.95)

196

*Embracing Each Other: Relationship as Teacher, Healer, and Guide.* By Drs. Hal and Sidra Stone. In this compassionate guide to understanding and improving relationships, the authors expand on their first book, *Embracing Our Selves*. In this new work, they concentrate on using the Psychology of Selves and their remarkable Voice Dialogue method to heal wounded relationships. This book teaches us to accept and appreciate the dance of the selves so that every relationship can become a source of never-ending fascination and growth. (Tradepaper $10.95)

*Embracing Our Selves: The Voice Dialogue Manual.* By Drs. Hal and Sidra Stone. This is the highly acclaimed, groundbreaking work that explains the Psychology of Selves and the Voice Dialogue method. Internationally renowned psychologists Hal and Sidra Stone first developed the Voice Dialogue process in the early 70s. Through worldwide workshops and retreats, they have refined the process to the point where it is now considered one of the most effective techniques in psychology today. (Tradepaper $12.95)

*Living in the Light: A Guide to Personal and Planetary Transformation.* By Shakti Gawain, with Laurel King. This classic on developing intuition and using it as a guide in daily life shows you how to become attuned with the power of the universe and how to recognize and act on your intuition. You'll learn how to create a relationship with a Higher Power, become a creative channel, balance work and play, create better health, have a positive relationship with money, and more! (Tradepaper $11.95)

*Living in the Light Workbook.* By Shakti Gawain. Shakti has created this companion workbook to *Living in the Light* to help us explore our intuition and trust our feelings more fully and deeply. This workbook includes 43 new exercises and meditations to help develop intuition, explore unconscious beliefs, create fulfilling relationships, and achieve better health. (Tradepaper $11.95)

*Maps to Ecstasy: Teachings of an Urban Shaman.* By Gabrielle Roth. Gabrielle Roth is a unique healer—a shaman for the modern American culture. In this book, she teaches us how to heal our wounded psyches by breaking out of our addictive cycles. She invites us out of our complacent, unfulfilled lives, and reconnects us to the vital, energetic core of our being. This practical program helps us reconnect with our primal knowledge, awaken our latent shamanic powers, and transform our daily lives into sacred art. (Tradepaper $10.95)

*Notes from My Inner Child: I'm Always Here.* By Tanha Luvaas. Many books have been written about the importance of reconnecting with our inner child. Here is the first book ever written *by* the inner child. As Shakti Gawain said about this book, It's "a must for all those who want to know more about the wise, wonderful, and magical inner child." (Tradepaper $8.95)

*Passion to Heal: The Ultimate Guide to Your Healing Journey.* By Echo Bodine. The author offers a unique and comprehensive exploration of the emotional healing process and how it affects our physical health, with powerful journal exercises to guide you to vibrant well-being on physical, emotional, mental, and spiritual levels. Echo combines the power of her experience as a healer with the vast array of alternative health-care practices to demystify the healing journey for the reader. (Tradepaper $14.95)

*The Path of Transformation: How Healing Ourselves Can Change the World.* By Shakti Gawain. In this powerful book, Shakti brings us an inspiring and provocative message for the 90s and the new millennium. She proposes that the solutions to our personal and planetary crises reside within each one of us and are truly within our reach. This book offers clear and effective steps for integrating all levels of our being and truly changing the world. (Tradepaper $11.95)

*Return to the Garden: A Journey of Discovery.* By Shakti Gawain. In this fascinating book, Shakti shares both her personal story, revealing the challenges inherent in a quest for self-discovery, and her vision of the future—a world in which ancient wisdom and modern technological intelligence have been combined, allowing us to live on earth in a natural and balanced way. She also shares many exercises, meditations, and rituals that have helped her to live in accordance with simple, universal principles. (Tradepaper $11.95)

*The Revelation: A Message of Hope for the New Millennium*. By Barbara Marx Hubbard. The author, whom R. Buckminster Fuller called "the best-informed human now alive regarding futurism"—turns to the prophetic visions recorded in the biblical book of Revelation to give us an astonishingly clear map for addressing today's problems. (Tradepaper $16.95)

*The Shadow King: The Invisible Force That Holds Women Back*. By Sidra Stone, Ph.D. Dr. Stone shows women how to discover the *inner* voice of the patriarchy, how to separate from it, and what women can do to reclaim their natural authority, dignity, and power while remaining feminine. (Tradepaper $12.95)

*The Turtle Tattoo: Timeless Tales for Finding and Fulfilling Your Dreams*. By Margaret Olivia Wolfson. In this book, the author, a professional storyteller herself, has gathered together allegories and tales that have moved women and men to achieve happiness and success for centuries. With lively discussions and instructions for applying the wisdom of these stories in our own lives, this book becomes a delightful adventure in actualizing our fondest dreams and aspirations. (Hardcover $14.95)

*What Women & Men Really Want: Creating Deeper Understanding & Love in Our Relationships*. By Aaron Kipnis, Ph.D., and Elizabeth Herron, M.A. What would we discover about male-female relationships if a group of men and women went into the wilderness together for several days to explore their gender differences? This fascinating book, which reads like a fast-paced novel, tells what happened on that excursion. (Tradepaper $12.95)

*Write from the Heart: Unleashing the Power of Your Creativity*. By Hal Zina Bennett. This is a book for everyone who loves books, words, and the dream of being a writer. Written in a warm, personal style, this book identifies the three key creative resources within each of us and tells how to access them through writing journals, poetry, fiction, and nonfiction. (Tradepaper $11.95)

## Audiocassettes

*Developing Intuition.* Shakti Gawain expands on the ideas about intuition she first discussed in *Living in the Light.* She explains what intuition is, how to connect with it, how to distinguish it from feelings, and why it is important that we make a conscious effort to develop it. (One audiocassette $10.95)

*The Four Levels of Healing.* On these inspiring audiocassettes—the first part of the *Journey to Wholeness Meditation Series*—Shakti Gawain shares her practical wisdom and guides you in powerful meditations that take you on your own journey to wholeness. She explains that our lives consist of four levels—spiritual, mental, emotional, and physical. To be whole, we need to heal and balance all four of these aspects. (Two-tape set $14.95)

*Living in the Light: A Guide to Personal and Planetary Transformation.* Shakti Gawain reads her classic work on how to develop intuition and use it as a guide to living your life. Learn how to become attuned with the creative power of the universe! (Two-tape set $15.95)

*The Path of Transformation: How Healing Ourselves Can Change the World.* Shakti Gawain reads her bestselling work, in which she confronts our global healing crisis and addresses what each of us can do individually to save our planet. (Two-tape set $15.95)

For more information on our company, please contact us at:

Nataraj Publishing
P.O. Box 2430
Mill Valley, CA 94942

**To place an order, call: (800) 949-1091**

# Praise for: The Shadow King

"Our task at hand, as we approach the 21st century, is to disengage from this depleting and damaging force known as the Inner Patriarch. In The Shadow King, Sidra Stone compassionately reveals the inner struggles that both women and men undergo in their dialogue with and taming of this force. Every page is vibrantly filled with Sidra's warmth, humor, and caring. With her assured guidance, we learn how to 'work with' this primal power, rather than to be its casualty."

–Cathleen Rountree, Author - The Heart of Marriage and On Women Turning 50

"Reading Sidra Stone's book The Shadow King was a mind-blowing experience. It gave me insight and understanding about my deep relationship to men and success in the world. It provides a process that gives me the tools to continue to learn and grow."

–Marsha Mason, Actress

"In Stone's hands, the Inner Patriarch is rightly understood as an energy that once recognized consciously and engaged creatively, can be harnessed in a positive way."

–Richard Moss, Author - The I That Is We, The Second Miracle

"Speaking of the importance of women as leaders in this new time is vital to a world so much in need of balancing the feminine with the masculine. Sidra's courage in sharing this wonderful work can help us fulfill the charge we all carry—to make a positive difference in our world."

–Brooke Medicine Eagle, Author - Buffalo Woman Comes Singing

"Long ago my teacher had me look into a pond as he stirred my reflections around in the water. Sidra Stone has stirred up the waters of the unknown in her new book The Shadow King. Her commitment to well-being for all living things along with her sensitive perception and non-judgmental way of showing us how to recognize, separate and reclaim this extremely powerful energy is truly a prayer answered for all humankind. Just read it and contemplate your life!"

–Marcellus 'Bear Heart' Williams, Author - The Wind I ' '

# What People Are Saying About The Shadow King:

"After reading this phenomenal book, my life will never be the same. I finally understand why I have been absolutely paralyzed by anxiety and doubt at times in my life, unable to move forward in my work, certain situations and relationships. By acknowledging the part of me I know as the Inner Patriarch, I have been able to free myself from it and to learn that its gift is a concern for my protection and safety. Dr. Stone is on the cutting edge of self-transformational work."
–Reverend Mary Ann Dickinson - Boulder, CO

"This book brings a revolution in consciousness. In my private practice, the Inner Patriarch provides an essential key to unlocking the doors of business power, successful relationships, and modern spirituality. In my personal experience, integrating the Inner Patriarch has brought my dreams to life—and has enhanced my relationships a thousand-fold!"
–Judith Hendin, Counselor - Wilkes-Barre, PA

"The work Sidra has done with the Inner Patriarch has saved my life. This work is creating real change for the future of young women today. I feel blessed that I'm able to pass this on to my daughter."
–Donna James, Businesswoman, Facilitator - Vancouver, BC

"About 20 years ago, I read that 'it is hard to fight an enemy that has outposts in your head' in an article about the women's movement. It made such logical sense that many of our limitations were self-imposed, but it was hard to know exactly what to do about that back then. Sidra Stone's work, The Shadow King, finally provides a map of those outposts and, better still, offers an effective way to navigate and alter them so that the Inner Patriarch can become an advocate rather than an adversary in women's everyday lives."
–Nancy D. Young, Ph.D., Clinical Psychologist - Orange, CA

"The gift of awareness and understanding of this 'Shadow King' has given me a profound sense of freedom. After working with Dr. Sidra Stone, I have for the first time in my life experienced the kind of intimacy that is possible once the Inner Patriarch lets go and allows true feelings and vulnerability to surface. This work is changing the way people look at relationships."
–John Nutting, Relationship Counselor - Brisbane, Australia

"I struggled against the outer patriarchy for years as a politically active feminist, and finally when I met my own Inner Patriarch I understood why it so often seemed I was taking one step forward and two steps back. On the outside I argued rights for women, but inside my own head was a man setting strict limits on what I could dare for myself. Like so many women I'm great at starting things, but successful completion is hard because it means being big, being out there in the world, competing with men. Now I realize there is an anxious father inside of me who worries that I'll fall on my face, be rejected, abandoned, hurt, left destitute, etc. He's an old-fashioned guy who thinks I should be taken care of by a wealthy husband and stay safely out of the limelight. Thanks to this work, I have fortunately learned that when I embark on a new project and start to feel his anxiety well up inside me, I can listen to him, reassure him and actually enlist his help."
–Mirium Dyak, Poet, Teacher, Business Woman, Counselor - Seattle

"When I separated from this oppressive voice, I dared to state what I want and set my own limits. I got a new self-confidence and a whole new and delightful relationship with my husband."
–Liv Dons Samset - Oslo, Norway

"As the Inner Patriarch of a woman makes her ashamed and defensive, a strong Inner Matriarch in a man can unconsciously create the same feelings and reactions. For men who have difficulty relating to other men, or who feel easily shamed by women, Sidra's chapter on the Inner Matriarch is a must-read. Learning to separate from my Matriarch has allowed me for the first time in over 40 years to feel totally O.K. about being a 'guy'. Sidra's work advances an enlightened consciousness in both women and men."
–Greg Haraldson, Facilitator and Businessman - Calgary, Canada

"Meeting my inner patriarch was truly transformational. As soon as I heard his voice, I knew he had been sabotaging me for years."
–Robin Gale, Psychotherapist, Trainer - Melbourne, Australia

"There are magic moments in working with oneself and with others when the feeling of liberation and expansion are palpable, and oh, so fulfilling! It has been my joy and privilege to live many of those moments, thanks to Sidra's gifts to mankind: the understanding and the experience of the Inner Patriarch, and the subsequent flight to freedom from its unconscious power."
–Manuela Terraluna, Teacher, Counselor - Parma, Italy

"Many of us have learned to manage that part of ourselves who either readily succumbs to or rebels against outside authority. What we have not learned is that there is an inner authority figure which is a much more demanding task-master than anything outside. This Inner Patriarch as described in Sidra Stone's book is so brilliantly examined that we cannot help but explore the rules and constraints we impose on ourselves and stand up to the fact that we can and must harness our power as women."

–Kathryn Altman, Businesswoman, Teacher,
Consultant - Mill Valley, CA

"Unidentified, unacknowledged and disowned, the Inner Patriarch is the agent of our imprisonment. It constantly undermines us as women and thwarts our creative and sensual expression. Objectified and reclaimed, it can, among other things, become a powerful ally in our quest to give form and structure to our endeavors and help us set boundaries in our relationships."

–Valma Granich - Perth, Australia

"Putting her finger on the Inner Patriarch, Sidra is helping to make this elusive force in me more conscious so that I don't have to believe its authoritative words as the truth. When I was writing my book, I could feel his presence standing over my shoulder telling me I have nothing worth sharing. Without having known him, it might have felt like God's truth to me and stopped me from going further."

–Tanha Luvaas, MFCC, Counselor, Facilitator - Chico, CA

"Working with the Inner Patriarch has opened the door to a whole new understanding of myself and my relationships. I experienced how this energy keeps me locked into certain patterns in my relationships with men and how powerfully it stands between me and other women."

–Ana Barner, Businesswoman - Wellington, New Zealand

"The Shadow King is a must-read manual for anyone wanting to discover a new key to an old block that thousands of years of Patriarchy has instilled deep within each of us! I am grateful for Sidra's clear vision into the underpinnings of such a significant and previously unrecognized force of cultural conditioning."

–Deborah Morris, LCSW, Psychotherapist and
Consultant - Mill Valley, CA